THE BORN-AGAIN PHENOMENON
(A COVER-UP FOR HERESY)

by
W. E. Best

South Belt Assembly of Christ
10603 Blackhawk Blvd.
P. O. Box 34904
Houston, Texas 77234-4904 USA

Scripture quotations in this book designated
"NASB" are from the NEW AMERICAN
STANDARD BIBLE, © 1960, 1962, 1963,
1968, 1971, 1972, 1973, 1975, and 1977 by the
Lockman Foundation, and are used by permis-
sion. Those designated "translation" are by the
author and taken from the Greek Text. All others
are from the King James Bible.

This book is distributed by the
W. E. Best Book Missionary Trust
P. O. Box 34904
Houston, Texas 77234-4904 USA

CONTENTS

Section II

The Objective Aspect Of Life
John 3:9-15

Section III

Results Of Subjective And Objective Life
John 3:16-21

INTRODUCTION

There is no portion of Scripture used more, abused worse, and understood less than John 3:1-21. Theologically, this passage of God's Holy Word is used by denominationalists and nondenominationalists to represent various views concerning soteriology, the science of salvation. Three major systems of belief concerning salvation encompass most professing believers, but all are not true believers. These are the three major systems: (1) baptismal regeneration, (2) faith regeneration, and (3) Spirit regeneration.

Heresy cloaked in Biblical language remains heresy. Because of the nature of this subject, the correct term is heresy, not error. Scriptural terminology is used by many to teach the opposite of what Scripture actually affirms. Although the term "born again" is Biblical, it is being used by politicians to get votes, by athletes who are disobedient concerning the Lord's day, by local assemblies who attract crowds with entertainers, and by religious leaders who peddle the word of God for profit. Hence, the so-called "born-again Christian" phenomenon has become the fastest growing cult in America.

In no way can John 3:1-21 teach so many divergent views on the science of man's deliverance from the penalty and condemnation of sin. The idea that God's word which has been permanently established in heaven and permanently given (Ps. 119:89; Jude 3) can mean different things to different people is ludicrous. Such thinking deserves ridicule because it is an attack on the veracity of God. Nothing is given in time but what was purposed in eternity. Thus, the order for which informed Christians contend is the relation between cause and effect. This order is confirmed in creation (John 1:1-3), redemption (John 3:14-16; Acts 2:23), and regeneration (John 3:1-16).

We shall see, in our striving to accomplish a knowledgeable study of John 3:1-21, how little that people in general understand passages that are so familiar to professing Christians. This portion of Scripture will be explored by considering the following truths:

1. Regeneration is necessary because of degeneration (the state of being degenerate or depraved). Regeneration is God's inward work of grace by the agency of the Holy Spirit in which He implants the principle of spiritual life in the soul.

2. The purpose of regeneration is to produce an outward act of turning to God in a conversion experience that causes one to keep on turning to God in conversion experiences. Thus, the inward change of life finds expression in an outward change that keeps changing until the final change. Regeneration, a single and completed act, is never repeated. Conversion is the beginning of a progressive and endless holy life until we shall be made like Jesus Christ. Regeneration is exclusively God's act on the passive sinner; conversion is the act of the regenerated person by the power of the inward principle of life. Subsequent to God's drawing, the one drawn follows Him.

3. Distinction is made between the regenerate, those who love the light, and unregenerate, those who hate the light (John 3:17-21). One can never be becoming like Christ unless he is first existing in Christ (John 1:12, 13).

SECTION I

THE SUBJECTIVE ASPECT OF LIFE
John 3:1-8

1

A DEPRAVED RELIGIONIST

> Now there was a man of the Pharisees, his name
> Nicodemus, a ruler of the Jews; this man came
> to Him by night and said to Him: Rabbi, we have
> known that you have come as a teacher from
> God; for no one is able to do these miracles that
> you are performing, unless God is with him.
> —John 3:1-2 (translation)

Although Nicodemus was a high ranking official of the
Jews, he was a depraved religious Pharisee. Since
Nicodemus' (compound noun—*nike*, victory and *demos*, people or crowd) name means "conqueror of the populace," he was
more than a master of a synagogue. He was a member of the
Sanhedrin, the supreme ecclesiastical and civil tribunal, which
was the final court for the interpretation and enforcement of the
Jewish law. The Pharisees were zealous for their religious sect,
which began soon after the return of the Jews from Babylonian
captivity. Therefore, they not only rejected the message of
Christ's forerunner, John the Baptist (Matt. 21:25-27; Luke 7:29,
30), but they also became Christ's greatest enemies (John 8).

The Pharisees were separatists who had their own interpretation of the Scriptures. Like many religionists today, the Pharisees had their own code of morals and placed great emphasis on external evidences of their religious piety. In fact, they made void the sacred Scriptures by their own traditions (Mark 7). No wonder Christ's strongest language of denunciation was against them (Matt. 23).

All we know about Nicodemus is recorded in John 3:1-12, 7:50, and 19:39. Nicodemus did not know he was a lost sheep when he came to Jesus Christ at night. The context will settle the differing views concerning the reason the Pharisee came at night. His first statement betrayed him: "...Rabbi [Master or Teacher], we have known [perfect active indicative of *oida*] that you have come [perfect active indicative of *erchomai*] as a teacher from [*apo*, ablative of source from or out of] God..." (John 3:2—translation). The first person plural "we" gave the impression that he had nothing personal at stake but that he was speaking on behalf of the Sanhedrin. If that was true, why did he come at night? Some think his coming at night manifested cowardice. Others think it was the best time for Nicodemus to have a conversation without the interruption of the normal activities of the day. The two perfect tense verbs give credence to the fact that Nicodemus had known for some time that Jesus Christ was a teacher who had come from God. Furthermore, he was in a state of knowing that Christ's works were of the nature that apart from God's presence He would be unable to perform them.

The chapter division would be more fitting beginning with John 2:23. Although many believed when they saw the miracles Jesus Christ was performing [imperfect active indicative of *poieo*] at the passover in Jerusalem, Christ was not entrusting [imperfect active indicative of *pisteuo*] Himself to them (John 2:24), because He "was knowing" [imperfect active indicative of *ginosko*] what was in man (John 2:25).

We determine the character of trees by their fruit, but Christ knows the very roots of the trees. Therefore, there are believers and there are believers. Faith may be sincere but superficial (human). It may be brought into exercise by miracles or circumstances, but it will disappear with the disappearance of the things that brought it into exercise. Christ cannot entrust Himself to a person who exercises that kind of faith, because He knows he is a "stony ground hearer," and his faith is only temporary. "And the ones on the rock are those who when they hear receive the word with joy; and these have no root, who believe for a brief time and in time of trial become apostates" (Luke 8:13—translation).

Nicodemus came to Jesus Christ at night as an anxious inquirer; however in the light of the context, his coming was motivated by the miracles that the Lord Jesus was performing. His coming cannot be classified with "Come to me all the ones laboring [present active participle of *kopiao*] and having been loaded with burdens [perfect passive participle of *phortidzo*, to load with a burden], and I shall give you rest" (Matt. 11:28—translation). The proud Pharisee addressed Jesus Christ as "Rabbi" thus placing himself on the same level with the Lord. He was saying that we Rabbis have known what you are doing as a Rabbi. This manner of address leaves little doubt that Nicodemus did not at that time know who Jesus Christ really was, even though he acknowledged that God was associated with Him.

The questions Nicodemus asked prove he was not regenerated when he came to Jesus Christ. "How is a man being able to be born being old?" (John 3:4a—translation). "Can he be able to enter into his mother's womb a second time and be born?" (v. 4b—translation). "How can these things come into being?" (John 3:9b—translation). Like Nicodemus, many come to Christ in order to ask questions rather than to listen. The depravity of their hearts is revealed in their interrogation. Nicodemus' questions revealed (1) how the natural man is unable to understand spiritual things (I Cor. 2:14), (2) how far a person can be advanced in worldly wisdom (including religious wisdom) and be spiritually ignorant, and (3) how one can belong to organized religion and know nothing about saving grace. This is characteristic of the great majority of religionists. They are not only lost but they are also like the Pharisees, Christ's worst enemies.

Jesus Christ did not reply to Nicodemus, because He was no ordinary rabbi speaking to another ordinary rabbi. He was God who came as the Teacher. Jesus Christ needs no one to witness concerning man, since He knows what is in man [generic use of *anthropos*, mankind] (John 2:25). Knowing Nicodemus' condition, Christ addressed him as an unregenerate man: "Jesus answered and said to him: Truly truly I am telling you, unless one may be born [*gennethe*, aorist passive subjunctive of *gennao*, to be born] from above [*anothen*, an adverb meaning from above], he is not able [*dunatai*, present passive indicative of *dunamai*, can, be able to, or able to do] to understand [*idein*, aorist active infinitive of *horao*, to see or understand] the kingdom of God" (John 3:3—translation).

The adverb *anothen* is used several ways in the New Testament: (1) upper room (Mark 14:15; Luke 22:12), (2) the top (Matt. 27:51; Mark 15:38; John 19:23), (3) from the very first (Luke 1:3), (4) again—a favorite translation by many (John 3:3, 7; Gal. 4:9), (5) from above (John 3:31; 19:11; James 1:17; 3:15, 17), (6) from the beginning (Acts 26:5). In all the references in John, "from above" makes good theology (John 3:3, 7, 31; 19:11, 23). "Born from above" of John 3:3 and 7 shows that the new life comes down from God, and it effects a complete and radical change in the elect who have been raised out of spiritual death, which is the result of their depravity.

Depravity is denied by the intelligentsia of this world order and by many religionists in professing Christendom. Among the religionists, the following statements are often heard or read to try to refute the truth of depravity: (1) Adam sinned only in his own person, and there is no reason that God should impute Adam's sin to infants. (2) That which we have by birth cannot be the evil of sin. (3) Sin must be voluntary or it cannot be sin. (4) That one should be accounted guilty of a sin that is not his own is inequitable. (5) God cannot in justice appoint anyone to hell for original sin. (6) The old fatalistic view of God's relationship to man is fading away. The new view sees God as giving to man the potential for working out his own destiny. (7) Man is not so corrupted by sin that he cannot of himself believe to the saving of his soul. (8) The sinner can be saved anytime he desires to believe, because today is the day of salvation. (9) Since the sinner is commanded to believe, he is not so dead and passive that he cannot believe. (10) Names are written and sealed in heaven at the point of faith. Hence, faith, regeneration, and justification all take place simultaneously.

In contrast to the preceding statements in which depravity is refuted, depravity signifies the following truths concerning what man is by nature:

1. He is spiritually dead: "And you existing [present active participle of *eimi*, to be or to exist] dead in your trespasses and sins" (Eph. 2:1—translation). Before the Ephesians were made alive together with Christ (Eph. 2:5), they were existing in a continuous state of spiritual death.

2. He is darkness: "For you were [imperfect active indicative of *eimi*] formerly darkness..." (Eph. 5:8—translation). This is not what unregenerate people do, but what they are by nature. "Being the ones who have been darkened [perfect passive participle of *skotidzo*, to be or to become darkened]

in their reasoning [*dianoia*, mind, reasoning, understanding, or thought], having been alienated from [perfect passive participle of *apallotrioo*, to be aliens or foreigners] the life of God, through the ignorance being in them, on account of the hardness of their heart" (Eph. 4:18—translation).

3. He is mortal. Physical death is the house appointed for all living (Gen. 3:19; Job 30:23; Rom. 5:12-14; Heb. 9:27).

The verb *dunamai*, which means can, be able to, or be capable of, is used in its present passive indicative inflected form (*dunatai*) in the following verses to further establish the truth of the spiritual inability of those who are spiritually dead; the ability or capability in each verse is negated by the Greek adverb *ou*. The sinner is unable to (1) understand the kingdom (John 3:3), (2) enter the kingdom (John 3:5), (3) come to Christ (John 6:44), or (4) understand spiritual things (I Cor. 2:14). In case the negated *dunamai* is not enough to convince religionists, consider the following Scriptures: "There is not one who understands, there is not one who seeks after God" (Rom. 3:11—translation). "And you are not willing to come to Me that you may have life" (John 5:40—translation). "The one who is of God is hearing the words of God; you therefore are not hearing, because you are not of God" (John 8:47—translation). "But you are not believing, because you are not from My sheep. My sheep are hearing my voice, and I know them, and they are following Me" (John 10:26, 27—translation).

2

A PASSIVE SINNER

> Jesus answered and said to him: Truly truly I am
> telling you, unless one may be born from above,
> he is not able to understand the kingdom of God.
> —John 3:3 (translation)

In the study of the total spiritual inability of the unregenerate, one cannot ignore the passivity of those who are not
born of God. The passive voice of the Greek verb *gennao*
(may be born) in John 3:3 represents the subject as the
recipient of the action, signifying that the subject is being
acted upon. If the subject were a participant in regeneration,
it would be in the middle voice. Furthermore, if the subject
could regenerate himself, the action would be in the active
voice. Anytime man is associated with the active or middle
voice used with *sodzo* or *gennao*, there is no connection with
one's being made spiritually alive. This brings us to the
importance of Christ's first statement to Nicodemus in John
3:3.

Jesus Christ gave no instruction to Nicodemus concerning

how he could be born of God. But how many times have we heard preachers and others tell people how they can be born again? They are doing something the Savior Himself never did throughout His personal ministry. Although Christ used the imperative (command) when He said, "repent" (Matt. 4:17; Mark 1:15) and "believe" (Mark 1:15; 5:36), He never commanded anyone to be born from above, be regenerated, or be quickened. Distinction must be made between the new birth and faith. Christ's first statement to Nicodemus was, "Truly truly I am telling you, unless one may be born [*gennethe*, aorist passive subjunctive of *gennao*, to be born] from above, he is not able [present passive indicative of *dunamai*, is able, negated by the adverb *ou*] to understand [*idein*, aorist active infinitive of *horao*, to see, observe, or understand] the kingdom of God" (John 3:3—translation). The subjunctive mood of the verb *gennao* is in the passive voice. The definition of the passive voice should be considered from two points of view: (1) The subject of the verb is inactive, and (2) the subject is acted upon by someone else. The following is a list of the verses where the passive voice of the verb *gennao* is used:

1. John 1:13—"Who not out of bloods nor out of the will of the flesh nor out of the will of man but out of God were born [*egennethesan*, aorist passive indicative]" (translation).

2. John 3:3—"...Truly truly I am telling you, unless one may be born [*gennethe*, aorist passive subjunctive]..." (translation).

3. John 3:5—This is the same as verse 3.

4. John 3:6—"That which has been born [*gegennemenon*, perfect passive participle] out of the flesh is flesh, and that which has been born

[*gegennemenon*, perfect passive participle] out of the Spirit is spirit" (translation).

5. John 3:7—"Do not wonder because I said to you: It is necessary for all of you to be born [*gennethenai*, aorist passive infinitive] from above" (translation).

6. John 3:8—"The Spirit is breathing where He desires, and you are hearing His voice, but you have not understood where He is coming from and where He is going; thus is everyone who has been born [*gegennemenos*, perfect passive participle nominative masculine singular] out of the Spirit" (translation).

7. I John 2:29—"If you may know absolutely that He is righteous, you know also that everyone doing righteousness has been born [*gegennetai*, perfect passive indicative] out of Him" (translation).

8. I John 3:9—"Everyone who has been born [*gegennemenos*, perfect passive participle nominative masculine singular] out of God does not practice sin, because his seed is remaining in him; and he is not able to be sinning, because he has been born [*gegennetai*, perfect passive indicative] out of God" (translation).

9. I John 5:1—"Everyone believing that Jesus is the Christ has been born [*gegennetai*, perfect passive indicative] out of God, and everyone loving the One who gave birth is loving the one who has been born [*gegennemenon*, perfect passive participle accusative masculine singular]

out of God" (translation).

10. I John 5:4—"...because everything that has been born [*gegennemenon*, perfect passive participle nominative neuter singular] out of God is overcoming the world; and this is the victory overcoming the world, our faith" (translation).

11. I John 5:18—"We have known [perfect active indicative of *oida*] that everyone who has been born [*gegennemenos*, perfect passive participle nominative masculine singular] out of God does not practice sin, but the one having been born [*gennetheis*, aorist passive participle] out of God is guarding himself, and the wicked one cannot harm him" (translation).

This list of Scriptures proves that regeneration (born out of God) is the exclusive work of the sovereign God upon the passive sinner. To deny that the sinner is completely passive to spiritual things is to deny depravity. Some argue that if man is totally unable to exercise his reasoning faculty and freedom of will and choice, he would be so insensible that he would not know it when he went to hell. They say that although the rich man of Luke 16:19-31 was totally unable to flee the torments of hades, he was not totally unable to exercise his will and choice for mercy, because he asked for mercy and relief. Their rationalization leads them to question, since this was done in hades, why can it not be done on earth? They quote Isaiah 1:18 to support their claim that the sinner exercises his reason before he is made as white as snow. Furthermore, their opinion is that the sinner must exercise freedom in order to come to the Lord before he finds rest (Matt. 11:28). They conclude that any person who says the sinner is totally incapable of repentance and faith reverses the order and does not understand the following things: (1) The sinner walks in sin (Eph. 2:1, 2). (2) He is dead and alive at the same time (I Tim. 5:6). (3) He may become dead to sin by grace without being a corpse (Rom. 6:11). (4) He is not insensitive while he is dead in sin, because he is able to reason and choose to leave the hog pen (Luke 15:11-32). (5) He is responsible to repent and believe while he is dead in sin (Mark 1:15). (6) Though dead in sin, the sinner can make a decision to live (Ezek. 18:31). (7) He is not destined to be regenerated apart from repentance and faith (Luke 7:50).

Biblical testimony is replete with evidences of complete depravity. So deep is original sin that as death came to Adam on account of his sin, death comes to all men because all have sinned (Rom. 5:17-19). Fallen man has become corrupt in all his ways; therefore, his whole nature moves in opposition to God. Corruption is evident throughout all of man's life, and it comes from the depths of his depraved heart. Life outside of Christ is in sin, guilt, lusts of the flesh, disobedience, hardness, and unrepentance and under the wrath of God. Apart from the grace of regeneration (born of God, born from above, new birth, made alive, or new creation), the sinner continues in a life of sin which results in his treasuring up wrath against the day of wrath and God's righteous judgment. His sinful existence does not stop at death: "The one acting unjustly let him act unjustly still, and the filthy one let him act filthily still..." (Rev. 22:11—translation).

Persons who believe that fallen man has the ability to make a one hundred and eighty degree turn—from going away from God to going to God—apart from grace is no different from those who believe there is a Divine spark within every man. Several years ago in a discussion on depravity between a liberal and an evangelical, they evidenced no difference in their beliefs. The liberal read a paper concerning "fanning the spark into a flame"; in reply, the evangelical quoted Ephesians 2:1 to prove there is no spark to fan. The liberal commended him on his reply and asked him if he believed man has the ability in himself to either accept or reject the gospel. The evangelical unhesitatingly answered in the affirmative. The liberal then asked what that ability is in man. When the evangelical answered that it is man's free will, the liberal smilingly retorted that the evangelical called it free will, and he called it the spark of goodness.

One must understand that man as a passive sinner is not a partner with God in regeneration. In contradiction to the Arminian concept, "God will save you if you will open the door and let Him come into your heart," the passive sinner does not play the decisive role in the new birth. Who opens whose heart for the truth? Scripture answers, "And a certain woman by name Lydia, a dealer of purple cloth of the city of Thyatira, who is worshipping God, was listening, whose heart the Lord opened to be paying close attention to the things being spoken by Paul" (Acts 16:14—translation). Thus, the Holy Spirit and not Paul's preaching enabled Lydia to receive the message which affected her understanding, emotion, and will to enable her to pay close attention.

The Arminian argument concerning the insensibility of the passive sinner is absurd. A person abandons common sense when he asserts that passivity would mean the rich man of Luke 16:19-31 would be so insensible that he would not know it when he went to hades. The Bible's use of the passive voice of Greek verbs, when they are used in reference to human beings, does not mean humans are absolutely insensible. The unregenerate person is physically alive but spiritually dead. Physically, the unregenerate person is not insensitive to his physical nature; but he is deprived of feeling of or sensation to spiritual things. In all fifteen places where the word *gennao* is used to signify born out of God, the living sinner was acted upon by God because he was passive concerning spiritual things. Although the sinner is insensitive to God's act of grace, like Lydia, he becomes sensitive to God's message and pays close attention to the things of God. Hence, when the unregenerate person is born of God, he goes from being passive to being active in and for spiritual things.

Concerning the exercise of the rich man's will and choice in hades, the answer is simple and crystal clear to everyone who has a spiritual mind. Those who believe in free grace do not deny that the sinner has a will; but his will is insensitive to spiritual things; therefore, it goes in only one direction, down, away from God (John 3:19, 20). Like water, it takes the path of no resistance. There is not a living sinner who would not like to be delivered from the torments of hell; but apart from grace, he does not want to be delivered from his sins which he loves and in which he has pleasure. His desire for deliverance is not from his sins but from physical torture.

Let us now get a picture of the rich man in hades. There are three contrasts in Luke 16:19-31: (1) contrast in life (vv. 19-21), (2) contrast in death (v. 22), and (3) contrast in eternity (vv. 23-31). Consider only the part that some apply to teach the rich man exercised his will and choice in requesting mercy and relief from his torments (vv. 23-31). Being afraid of future punishment while one is living in time and the actual experience of torture in eternity vastly differ. Although the rich man is suffering the tortures of hades, in his request, he stated nothing about God, righteousness, or holiness. He expressed only that which is related to the physical and not the spiritual realm. This proves that his will and choice were concerned about one thing—the physical. Hence, the will of the rich man in hades is continuing its downward course away from God.

The sinner's exercising his reason before he can be made as white as snow is another blunder of Arminians. To whom were the words of Isaiah 1:16-20 spoken? God does not reason with the unreasonable. These words were not connected with either the preceding (vv. 10-15) or the following verses (vv. 21-27), but they apply to the remnant God had among the wicked. There is no mercy at the bar of justice, but there is at the throne of grace. "Come now, and let us reason together, saith the LORD: though your sins be as scarlet, they shall be as white as snow; though they be red like crimson, they shall be as wool" (Is. 1:18). This is similar to David's request, "Purge me with hyssop, and I shall be clean: wash me, and I shall be whiter than snow" (Ps. 51:7). God was telling the remnant to break off sins by repentance and then follow instruction. The instruction can be applied not only to David in Psalm 51, but also to the assembly (II Cor. 7:1).

Reason apart from grace is unreasonable in regard to spiritual things. The mind of the unregenerate is natural (I Cor. 2:14), fleshly (Col. 2:18), vain (Eph. 4:17, 18), and defiled (Titus 1:15). Can a depraved mind make sound spiritual judgments? If so, it would be like a bad fountain giving forth good water, and there would be no value in the Spirit of regeneration. If the sinner has the ability to discern both natural and spiritual things and by his own ability he chooses the spiritual, he does not hate good but evil, which is contrary to John 3:19-20. Scripture teaches that subsequent to the fall the sinner discerns the evil; on the other hand, the Christian has his senses exercised to discern both good and evil (Heb. 5:14).

The Hebrew verb for "reason" (*yakah*, to be right, demonstrate what is true, argue, decide, plead, reason, or rebuke) in Isaiah 1:18, the most familiar passage in the Old Testament, means to be right or demonstrate what is true. Some translate it, "let us debate our case in court." Suggesting this judicial sense has strong support in the light of Isaiah 11:1-4. These words were spoken to the prophet for the benefit of those whose reason had been made reasonable by grace. Thus, there was a remnant not so self-willed as to build a theological system which would say either less or more about God than He had said about Himself. To them, God revealed Himself, because they were able to rise above and beyond the comprehension of human reason.

Hypocrites boldly enter into dispute with God, but reason marks Christians as distinct from hypocrites. Christians understand that the proper function of reason in relation to faith is to receive God's truth, because grace provides for believers: "...weapons of warfare are not fleshly but powerful to God for the purpose of tearing down bulwarks, destroying sophistries [fallacious reasonings] and every high thing rising up against the knowledge of God, and taking captive every thought [*noema*, method, design, or plot] to the obedience of Christ" (II Cor. 10:4, 5—translation).

The Arminian argument that the sinner must exercise his free will to come to Christ before he can have rest is another denial of depravity. The statement in Matthew 11:28, "Come to Me all the ones laboring and having been loaded with burdens, and I shall give you rest" (translation), must be studied in the light of its immediate context. An important question is necessary at this point, who first comes to whom? Subsequent to the fall, Adam did not first come to the "LORD God"; but the "LORD God" came to the garden where Adam was hiding and called him (Gen. 3:8-10). The woman of Samaria did not first come to Christ; He came to her (John 4:4-30). Zacchaeus did not first come to Christ; Christ came to him (Luke 19:1-10). Christ said, "No one is able to come to me unless the Father who sent Me may draw him, and I shall raise him up on the last day" (John 6:44—translation).

One must learn what coming to Christ is not, prior to ascertaining what it is, in the light of Biblical evidence. (1) Coming to Christ is not a physical act, such as coming forward, raising the hand, going into an inquiry room, being baptized, etc. People will come as long as they think they can do something, but such physical acts can never achieve regeneration. (2) Coming to Christ is not an act of the mind, such as one's repeating the sinner's prayer or deciding for Christ. If this were all that is needed for the new birth, there would be no need for the regenerating work of the Holy Spirit. (3) Coming to Christ is not a mystical experience unfounded in Biblical truth, such as seeing a vision or hearing a voice. After considering the three things mentioned, we are reminded of people who, when asked if they are Christians, express such things as, "I made a decision to try Jesus"; "I saw Jesus in a vision"; or "I heard a voice."

Coming to Christ is a manifestation of regeneration. It is not in order to be born of God. Hence, coming to Christ is not a means of being born of God, but it evidences that the one coming has been born of God. Isaiah said, "HO! Every one who thirsts, come to the waters; And you who have no money come, buy and eat. Come, buy wine and milk Without money and without cost" (Is. 55:1 NASB). The three outstanding things in this text are water, wine, and milk. (1) Persons who are dissatisfied with all the formalism of religion thirst for the Spirit who cleanses like water. The Jews were acquainted with this terminology (Ezek. 36:25, 26). Such dissatisfaction and thirst are effects of regeneration. (2) Wine is a symbol of Divine joy: "And wine which makes man's heart glad..." (Ps. 104:15 NASB). At the wedding in Cana, the good wine was kept until the last (John 2:10). Christ's turning water into wine refutes transubstantiation, the teaching of Roman Catholicism. If wine after consecration by the priest looks and tastes like it did before consecration, how can they say it is the blood of Christ? The best wine kept for the last at the wedding represents the glory of regeneration, showing that the last state is better than the first. (3) Milk is the food for spiritual growth: "As newborn infants desire the uncorrupted spiritual milk, in order that you by it may grow" (I Pet. 2:2—translation).

Coming to Christ involves a recognition of need, a revelation of Christ, and a resignation of oneself. The recognition of need does not take place in the unsanctified reason of the unregenerate mind. The person who enjoys life that is not centered in Jesus Christ has never been made to feel the weariness of his continuous state of burdens. Furthermore, he will never become cognizant of such weariness as a result of sins until he has been made spiritually alive by the sovereign Spirit.

Since God never starts something He does not finish, Jesus Christ is made known to the one who has been made to feel the weariness of his sins. He comes in the power of the regenerating Spirit to Christ as a repentant person. "At that time Jesus answering said: I am praising you, Father, Lord of the heaven and of the earth, because you concealed these things from the wise and intelligent, and made them known to immature ones; Yes indeed, Father, because in this way it was pleasing in your sight. All things were delivered to Me by My Father, and no one fully knows the Son except the Father, nor does anyone fully know the Father except the Son and him to whom the Son desires to make known" (Matt. 11:25-27—translation). As the Father is a mystery made known to Jesus Christ, Christ is made known to faith which is the fruit of one's having been born of God. That which is outside the understanding of human reason is not outside the comprehension of God-given faith to the elect.

Trinitarian knowledge is made known to the elect. The Father knows the Son, and the Son knows the Father (Matt. 11:27). God knows the mind of the Spirit (Rom. 8:27), and the Spirit knows the depths of God (I Cor. 2:10). The elect know God experientially because Christ desires to make Himself known (Matt. 11:27). According to Scripture, this knowledge is not presumptuous: "And by this we are knowing [present active indicative of *ginosko*] that we have known [perfect active indicative of *ginosko*] Him, if we may keep His commandments. The one saying, I have known [perfect active indicative of *ginosko*] Him, and keeping not His commandments, is a liar, and the truth is not existing in this one" (I John 2:3, 4—translation). Verse 3 is positive, but verse 4 is contrapositive. Although verse 3 speaks of experiential knowledge, John did not hesitate to call the person a liar who is always saying and not doing and to tell him the truth did not exist in him. The apostle did not assert in the first two verses of this chapter that one must be sinless before he is knowledgeable of his relationship with God, but he did state that one must not presume that he is safe prior to the grace of God making him long to be sinless. One must resolve not to sin, but he must be able to recognize sin when he commits it. The Greek makes a clear distinction between committing an act of sin, "if anyone may sin [aorist active—point action—subjunctive]" (I John 2:1—translation), and habitually sinning, "he cannot be continually sinning [present active—continuous action—infinitive]" (I John 3:9—translation).

Jesus Christ never commands an unregenerate person, as He does a regenerate person, to take His yoke and learn from Him: "Take [aorist active imperative of *airo*, to take or carry] My yoke [*dzugos*, yoke or slavery] upon [*epi*, accusative of advantage] you and learn by experience [aorist active imperative of *manthano*, to learn by experience] from [*apo*, ablative of source] Me..." (Matt. 11:29—translation). Wearing Christ's yoke is a symbol of submission. In his various admonitions to Timothy, Paul said, "Let as many slaves as are under a yoke regard their own masters worthy of all honor, in order that the name of God and the teaching may not be blasphemed" (I Tim. 6:1—translation). If Christians who are under a yoke of slavery are to regard their masters worthy for the sake of God's honor, what about the yoke of Jesus Christ which is said by Him to be pleasant (*chrestos*, good, pleasant, or easy) (Matt. 11:30)? He has promised His people that He will never allow us to be tested beyond our ability to bear (I Cor. 10:13). Not only is Christ's yoke pleasant but His burden is easy to bear (*elaphros*, easy to bear or insignificant). In view of the honor which the Master of masters is due, the yoke and burdens of Christ are insignificant in comparison to the glory we shall have when we see our Savior and behold His glory. Christians find rest (*anapausis*, rest or relief) while bearing the yoke of a slave and continuously being loaded with burdens (Matt. 11:29). Believers are able to bear burdens while bearing the yoke of slaves because of the rest the Savior gives to every repentant and believing person. The compound verb, "I will cause you to rest" (*anapauso*, first person singular future active indicative of *anapauo*), in Matthew 11:28 is made up of the preposition *ana*, up, and the verb *pauo*, to stop or cease.

3

UNSANCTIFIED REASON

> Nicodemus says to Him: How is a man being able to be born being old? Can he be able to enter into his mother's womb a second time and be born? —John 3:4 (translation)

Christ's statement, "Unless one may be born from above, he is not able to understand the kingdom of God" (John 3:3—translation), prompted a question from the unsanctified reasoning of the Jewish Rabbi: "Nicodemus says to Him: How is a man able to be born being old? Can he be able to enter into his mother's womb a second time and be born?" (John 3:4—translation). The Lord Jesus only stated a fact without explanation, because regeneration is something which God alone can perform. Birth from above was as foreign to Nicodemus, the teacher from Israel, as it is to most people in professing Christendom.

The popularity of the statement "born again" proves it is not understood. If it were comprehended to be the exclusive work of God, it would not be popular. Born from above presupposes that man is so sinful and hopelessly depraved that he is incapable of understanding anything that is of a spiritual nature. This fundamental truth is obnoxious to the depraved reasoning, intellectualism, and philosophy of this world's wisdom.

The humanist, whether secular or religious, is appalled with the suggestion that he has nothing to do with determining his destiny. Since our subject is restricted to the context of a religious Pharisee, we shall stay within the bounds of professing Christendom for its application, keeping in mind that Jesus Christ gave no instructions as to what a person must do in order to be born from above (born of God). The reason is obvious, because man can do nothing to be born from above.

Religionists who equate being saved with being born again say John 3:1-16 teaches certain things that one must do in order to be saved. They affirm that salvation consists in a person's belief of these four things: (1) God loves him; (2) he is lost; (3) Christ died for him; and (4) God will save him on the condition that he believes on Jesus Christ as Savior. Although millions of young people, college students, and others have been led to make decisions for Christ on the basis of these four laws, the decisions are false and empty apart from regeneration (born from above). If a passive sinner needs no more than believing God loves him, admitting he is lost, saying Christ died for him, and then believing on Him, regeneration is unnecessary to give him a new nature. Only in the power of a new nature can one understand the truth of the gospel, be capable of repenting on account of his grief according to God who works repentance to salvation never to be regretted (II Cor. 7:9, 10), and believe on Christ with God-given faith (Eph. 2:8; Titus 1:1). Both repentance and faith are fruits of one who has been born out of God by the power of the Holy Spirit (John 3:8).

Many teach that in order for anyone to be born from above, he must first hear and believe the gospel. They believe in what is commonly called "gospel regeneration," indicating that the gospel, God's objective message, is essential to regeneration, which they claim is both God's and man's subjective work. Therefore, to them "born from above" must be determined in some way by the response of the person who has been exposed to the gospel. However, the act of the Holy Spirit, who gives life to the spiritually dead, is as distinct from the truth of the gospel as seeing is different from light. Did the sowing of the seed on good ground change the nature of the soil (Matt. 13:8, 23)? If the word of God regenerates, why does it not produce the same results in all who are exposed to it? The problem lies not in the nature of the gospel but in the nature of the human heart. As the seed sown did not change the nature of the soil, the gospel preached to sinners does not change the nature of their hearts. If their hearts have not been changed by the Spirit of grace, their response will be the same as that of the first three soils (Matt. 13:3-7, 18-22).

Some who claim to embrace the Reformed teaching of depravity, election, particular redemption, irresistible grace, and the perseverance of the saints, at the same time deny this teaching by saying the soul of man is not merely passive in regeneration. Their use of the adverb "merely" indicates the idea that the sinner is not entirely, wholly, or to the full extent depraved. To deny one or more of the previously mentioned truths is to deny all, because they all stand or fall together. Scripture teaches that the elect are involved in regeneration, but it does not teach that we participate in our being born from above. The passive voice of all the references where the verb *gennao* is used in connection with regeneration proves this. Therefore, no one can refute the Biblical truth that the sinner is passive in regeneration.

Those of the opinion that the sinner is not wholly depraved

insist that the sinner is active when he is persuaded by the gospel in the illuminating power of the Spirit. Since he does not have the Holy Spirit, how can the sinner be illuminated by the Spirit (John 14:17; Rom. 8:9)? Persons who espouse this view believe there is a work of the Holy Spirit in the sinner that comes short of regeneration. Their major so-called proof text is Hebrews 6:4-6. They claim that one of the pre-salvation ministries of the Holy Spirit is to enable sinners who come under the influence of the gospel to have a certain appreciation for salvation. Thus, they insist that those "who believe for a brief time and in time of trial become apostates" (Luke 8:13b—translation) have been enlightened. However, their so-called proof texts do not harmonize with the teaching of Scripture. God never starts a work in anyone that He does not finish (Phil. 1:6). Furthermore, the enlightenment of the sinner is purely objective, not subjective. God's Spirit's not always striving with men (Gen. 6:3) refers to His not striving through the objective message that is proclaimed (Acts 7:51-60).

The writer of Hebrews 6:4-6 dealt with supposition rather than fact in order to correct false ideas. (1) He called attention to those who have been enlightened (aorist passive participle of *photidzo*, to enlighten, make known, or reveal). Their enlightenment was once for all (adverb, *hapax*, once, one time, or once for all—see Heb. 9:26, 27, 28; 10:2; 12:26, 27; Jude 3, 5). (2) He referred to those who have tasted (aorist middle participle of *geuomai*, to taste or experience—see Matt. 16:28; Heb. 2:9). Did the disciples experience a foretaste of the coming kingdom? Did Jesus Christ experience death? (3) He mentioned those who have become (aorist passive participle of *ginomai*, to become) partakers (pronominal adjective accusative masculine plural of *metochos*, which is derived from the verb *metecho*, *meta*, with and *echo* to have; means to share or participate in, partake of, or be a partner with; used only 6 times—Luke 5:7; Heb. 1:9; 3:1, 14; 6:4; 12:8). The Hebrew Epistle references prove the actual spiritual experiencing of the Holy Spirit. (4) He pointed to those who have tasted (aorist middle participle of *geuomai*—see the second point) the good word (*hrema*, that which is being of God or has been uttered by the living voice) of God. "How sweet are thy words unto my taste..." (Ps. 119:103). Sight evidences the knowledge of faith, and taste describes the experience of faith. (5) He referred to those who have tasted the powers (noun accusative feminine plural of *dunamis*, power, strength, or authority) of the age that is about to come (present active participle of *mello*, to be about to, or to be on the point of a settled future).

If the previously described persons with their experiences have fallen away (aorist active participle of *parapipto*, a compound verb made up of the preposition *para*, beside, when used with the accusative case, and *pipto*, to fall or to fall to one's ruin or destruction), it is impossible (*adunatos*, adjective used as a noun which means impotent, weak, or impossible) to renew (present active infinitive of *anakainidzo*, to renew or restore) them again (adverb, *palin*, back or again—with a verb it means a second time) a second time to repentance. The writer stated a hypothesis to prove the impossibility of the falling away of one who has experienced the preceding things. A genuine repentance in a true conversion experience can never be repeated. However, the initial repentance, which is the fruit of regeneration, produces a repentant spirit that causes the converted person to continue to repent when he knows that by his acts of sin fellowship with the Father is broken.

Other Reformers have difficulty making a proper distinction between regeneration and conversion due to what they call the time lag. They affirm that regeneration and conversion seem to occur simultaneously, but they admit that faith is dependent on regeneration. They believe it is impossible to distinguish any time lapse between regeneration and conversion. Their explanation calls for the facts of natural birth. Reference is made to the birth of a child being first initiated by conception, and then the analogy is applied to regeneration. The sound of a gun that is shot and the target hit has been used to illustrate the impossibility of distinguishing any time lag. Although they recognize the truth of cause and effect, to them the sound of the gun and the hit target seem to be simultaneous. However, the problem with this illustration is in how it can apply to conception and birth. How can a shot gun and a hit target, which seem to be simultaneous, be reconciled with nine months of gestation before birth? Such a conclusion would mean that regeneration must take place nine months before birth or conversion. Students of Scripture must not presume that earthly illustrations are perfect analogies of spiritual truths.

The question of a time lag between regeneration and conversion has caused much controversy. Some insist that there is no warrant for the expectation of a time lag. Others believe one who is merely regenerated is not saved, because there is no such person. The opinion of others is that passivity in regeneration is fatalistic. The verse most frequently used by those who express the belief that regeneration is accomplished by the word, and that there is no time lag between regeneration and conversion is James 1:18—"Having been purposed [aorist passive participle nominative masculine singular of *boulomai*, to desire, be willing, decree, or appoint] He brought us forth [aorist active indicative of *apokueo*, give birth to, to be the cause of, or to bring forth] by a message of truth, resulting in our being a certain firstfruit of His creatures" (translation). The meaning is not difficult to ascertain in the light of the context. Compare the use of the verb in verse 15—"Then lust having conceived is bearing [present active indicative of *tikto*, bear, give birth to, or produce] sin, and sin having been fully formed brings forth [present active indicative of *apokueo*] death" (translation).

The theory of immediate (instant or without delay) regeneration does not deny that the new life imparted in being born of God is brought to light (manifested) by the word of God. As the infant in the womb contributes nothing to his conception, the passive sinner contributes nothing to his birth from above. The instrumental means in bringing forth life to light is the gospel of Jesus Christ. (See II Tim. 1:9, 10). The beginning of the new life is expressed by the passive verb *gennao*, which has already been considered in all its fifteen references. It is also declared by the verbs *ktidzo*, to create (Eph. 2:10; 4:24), and *dzoopoieo*, to make alive or to give life (Eph. 2:5; John 6:63; II Cor. 3:6). The means of bringing the given life to light is fully explained in the verses following the first eight verses of the third chapter of John.

4

BORN OF WATER AND SPIRIT

> Jesus responded: Truly truly I am saying to you,
> unless one may be born out of water and Spirit,
> he is not being able to enter into the kingdom of
> God. —John 3:5 (translation)

Subsequent to Nicodemus' ignorant questions—"How is a man being able to be born being old? Can he be able to enter into his mother's womb a second time and be born?" (John 3:4—translation)—"Jesus responded: Truly truly I am saying to you, unless one may be born out of water and Spirit, he is not being able to enter into the kingdom of God" (John 3:5—translation). The words "Truly truly" come from the Greek word *amen*. They were spoken by Jesus Christ alone and recorded only in the Gospel of John.

Since the majority of professing Christians are members of religious denominations that strongly support the doctrine of baptismal regeneration, one can expect criticism and debate when the subject of soteriology is discussed. Those who espouse this view are quick to say that John 3:5 is not teaching two births, one of water and one of the Spirit, but that Christ is teaching one birth which includes both water and the Spirit. They affirm that in John 3:5 it is incontrovertibly obvious that water means water, and it refers to Christian baptism.

Four major views of soteriology rely on John 3:5 as their proof text:

1. Baptismal regenerationists claim that God would not have said water if He had not meant water. They explain that baptism alone is not regeneration, but it is an essential part of the new birth.

2. Those who teach that water refers to one's physical birth and the Spirit applies to one's spiritual birth believe the context proves both births.

3. Many evangelicals say water is a symbol of the word of God which the Spirit uses in regeneration. They conclude that the only baptism implied here is the baptism in the Holy Spirit which is regeneration by the word of God (I Cor. 12:13; Eph. 5:26).

4. According to both text and context, Scripture teaches that born of water and Spirit in John 3:5 means the Spirit cleanses like water (Ezek. 36:25, 26).

The sincere professing believer should at this point understand the importance of coming to a definite conclusion on the teaching of John 3:5. This study will test our desire to know what Christ is actually teaching, and it will also test the foundation of our relationship to God through Jesus Christ by the Holy Spirit. We are now facing a subject that will challenge our study and meditation.

Nicodemus, a teacher of Israel, familiar with Old Testament Scripture, should have known the teaching of Ezekiel 36:25-26—"Then will I sprinkle clean water upon you, and ye shall be clean: from all your filthiness, and from all your idols, will I cleanse you. A new heart also will I give you, and a new spirit will I put within you: and I will take away the stony heart out of your flesh, and I will give you an heart of flesh." Verse 25 teaches that God justifies those He elects. Verse 26 teaches that regeneration is by God. Only one birth is referred to in John 3:5, and it is the birth out of God by the regenerating Holy Spirit. Neither two births, physical and spiritual, nor two baptisms, water and spirit, are taught here.

Baptismal regenerationists are too anxious to add baptism to water wherever they think it fits their doctrine. The ordinance of baptism is never expressed by the word "water" without additional words or context to demonstrate the fact of an ordinance. Since the Lord Jesus was discussing the birth from above, there was no place for the ordinance of baptism by human hands on earth in connection with it. Therefore, distinction must be made between regeneration, which is accomplished solely by the sovereign God, and God's ordinance of baptism, which should be obeyed by the person who has been converted by the gospel subsequent to his having been born out of God.

Consider the following contrasts between regeneration and baptism:

1. Regeneration is by the agency of the Holy Spirit; baptism is in water administered by the agency of a man of God.

2. Regeneration is the instantaneous operation of God; baptism must wait for both the baptizer and water.

3. Regeneration changes the nature of the heart; baptism

is the external manifestation of that change in an act of obedience.

4. The Spirit of regeneration is irresistible; baptism can be denied by the baptizer until regeneration is evidenced.

5. Regeneration takes place in the sphere of man's subconsciousness; baptism takes place in his consciousness.

6. Regeneration is the gift of life; baptism is an act of obedience of that life.

7. Regeneration gives a good conscience; baptism is the answer of that conscience.

8. Regeneration is not dependent on the gospel; baptism is dependent on the proclamation of the gospel.

9. Regeneration enables the recipient to put away the filth of the flesh; baptism does not put away the filth of the flesh.

10. Regeneration is the application of Christ's blood; blood always precedes water.

Some have been so anxious to show that John 3:5 does not teach baptismal regeneration that they have failed to consider the Greek text: "*ean me tis gennethe ex hudatos kai pneumatos*—unless one may be born out of water and Spirit." Since born out of water does not mean baptism, what does it signify? There is only one birth referred to in the text. The single preposition *ex* (*ek*) describes the single event. John did not place a second *ek* before "Spirit" as though he were describing two events. This singularity is established by the aorist tense, which signifies once born of water and Spirit. Conclusively, this verse teaches neither two births nor two baptisms—water and Spirit.

Others of the opinion that the only baptism in this verse is the baptism in the Spirit believe Spirit baptism takes place at regeneration. They declare that regeneration takes place when the believer is baptized into the body of Christ by means of the Holy Spirit (I Cor. 12:13), who cleanses the believer by the water of the word (Eph. 5:26). They imply that the verse teaches the washing of regeneration and renewal of the Holy Spirit of Titus 3:5. Thus, they claim John 3:5 teaches that "born of water" is the washing of regeneration, and the "Spirit" is the renewal of the Spirit.

Like those who accept the teaching of baptismal regeneration, those who hold the view that baptism in the Holy Spirit is regeneration are too anxious to add the word "baptism" to Spirit when it fits their doctrine. Since there are only seven references to baptism in the Spirit, all of which point to Pentecost, their adding baptism to Spirit in John 3:5 and equating it with I Corinthians 12:13, which does not refer to regeneration, is not justifiable. Being born out of the Spirit (regeneration) and Christ's baptizing the body of believers in the Spirit at Pentecost to empower them for service immensely differ. One is instantaneous, out of the source of the Spirit (John 3:8); and the other is by the agency of Jesus Christ in the sphere of the Spirit (I Cor. 12:13). In the first, the preposition *ek* (ablative of source) is used, and in the second the preposition *en* (locative of sphere) is used. "Born out of the Spirit" is individual, and "in the sphere of one Spirit we all were baptized into one body" was corporate (I Cor. 12:13; Acts 1:5, 8; 2:1-4).

Nicodemus had acknowledged that Jesus Christ had come from God and that God was with Him in His performance of miracles. Why then did he raise questions concerning the words which Christ spoke about being born from above? Christ's works, which Nicodemus recognized, were the confirmation of His message (Mark 16:20; John 5:36). Nicodemus' questions manifested the depravity of his heart. Only those who have experienced the mystery of Christ within can understand what is either said or written concerning regeneration (Matt. 11:25-27; John 6:45; I Cor. 2:12-16; I John 2:20-27). Subsequent to his questions in verse 4, Nicodemus, who was standing only on a religious rite, was subjected to the greatest refutation of synergism (joint action of agents) recorded in Holy Scripture (John 3:6-8).

Having completed our study of the differing views of John 3:5, we will conclude this section of John 3, which focuses on the subject of regeneration. In the Old Testament, God first said "live" (Ezek. 16:6) before He said "look" (Is. 45:22). The same order is given in John 3:1-16; life is necessary in order for one to see and embrace the Savior. After removing any religious rite on which Nicodemus stood, Christ said, "That which has been born out of the flesh is flesh" (John 3:6a—translation). The verb "has been born" is a perfect passive participle nominative neuter singular of *gennao*, which means a completed action in past time with a continuing state of being. Since a participle is a verbal adjective, which has the characteristics of both the verb and the adjective, we observe by the inflected form of the adjectival part that the participle functions as a substantive. Hence, the nominative neuter singular article (*to*) agrees with the nominative neuter singular adjectival part of the participle which literally signifies the human nature which has been born out of (*ek*, ablative of source) the flesh (ablative feminine singular of *sarx*) exists (present active indicative of *eimi*, to be or exist) as human nature (a predicative nominative feminine singular of *sarx*).

The Greek noun *sarx* is used 148 times in the New Testament in a variety of ways, a few of which follow:

1. Flesh is the soft substance consisting of fat and muscle of humans and animals: "All flesh is not the same flesh, but one of men, and another of animals, and another of birds, and another of fish" (I Cor. 15:39—translation).

2. Flesh speaks of the totality of what man is in human existence: "For by reason of the works of the law no flesh shall be justified before Him; for through law is full knowledge of sin" (Rom. 3:20—translation).

3. Flesh has reference to the peccable human nature of depraved man: "That which has been born out of the flesh is flesh" (John 3:6a—translation).

4. Flesh signifies Christ's impeccable human nature: "And the Word became flesh [became veiled in impeccable human nature]..." (John 1:14—translation). "And the angel responded to her: The Holy Spirit shall come upon you, and the power of the Highest shall fall upon you; for this reason also the holy thing being born shall be called, Son of God" (Luke 1:35—translation).

5. Flesh refers to the lower and temporary principle of sin in the Christian: "But now no longer I work it out but the sin dwelling in me. For I have known that nothing good is dwelling in me [my sinful nature], for to be desiring is present with me, but to be accomplishing the good is not" (Rom. 7:17, 18—translation).

6. Flesh designates the marital relationship of man and woman: "And He said: for this cause a man shall leave father and mother and shall be joined to his wife, and the two shall exist as one flesh" (Matt. 19:5—translation).

The significance of the word flesh (*sarx*) that concerns us in our present study is the peccable or sinful nature in fallen man. The human nature which has been born out of sinful nature is in a continuous state of being depraved.

Sinful human nature can produce nothing but sinful human nature: "And Adam lived an hundred and thirty years, and begat a son in his own likeness, after his image..." (Gen. 5:3). "Behold, I was shapen in iniquity; and in sin did my mother conceive me" (Ps. 51:5). "Who can bring a clean thing out of an unclean? not one" (Job 14:4). Since sinful human nature subsequent to the fall is in a continuous state of sinfulness, it can in no way make any contribution to one's being born from above. Therefore, the passive sinner is at the mercy of the sovereign God of grace who chooses and saves whom He will. The leper who came to Jesus Christ spoke to Him according to the Scriptures: "And there comes a leper to Him begging Him and kneeling saying to Him, If you will you are able to cleanse me. And having been filled with compassion extended His hand and touched him and says to him: I am willing, you be cleansed at once. And immediately the leprosy left him, and he was cleansed" (Mark 1:40-42—translation).

Leprosy is a striking representation of the character and consequences of sin. Although the men in the synagogue had refused Divine sovereignty, the leper submitted to it. The event concerning the leper who came to Christ, recorded by Matthew, Mark, and Luke (Matt. 8:2-4; Mark 1:40-45; Luke 5:12-16) followed on the heels of what Christ said when He went forth from His testing subsequent to His baptism. While the people were marvelling at Christ's gracious words, He said, "Truly I am telling you: No prophet is accepted in his own hometown. But I am telling you about reality, many widows were in Israel in the days of Elijah, when the heaven was shut up for three years and six months, when great famine came over all the land, and to not one of them was Elijah sent except to Sarepta of Sidon to a widow woman. And many lepers were in Israel in the time of Elisha the prophet, and not one of them was cleansed except Naaman the Syrian" (Luke 4:24-27—translation). A sermon on grace in general will be tolerated by any religious institution; however, a message on grace in particular is hated by everyone who embraces the synergistic concept of soteriology. Proof of this is found in the reaction by the religionists in the synagogue who heard what Christ said: "And all in the synagogue hearing these things were filled with rage" (Luke 4:28—translation).

Although the leper did not doubt Christ's ability to heal his leprosy, he was not sure at this point in his untutored mind that God willed to heal him. Here is where the Greek gives help which cannot be seen so plainly in most English translations. The third class condition, which expresses a probable future condition, of "If [*ean*, conjunction used with the subjunctive mood verb] you are willing [*theles*, present active subjunctive of *thelo*, to will or desire]" (Luke 5:12—translation) indicates that the leper's healing depended on God's will rather than the will of the leper. Do you suppose this leper had heard about Christ's saying in the synagogue shortly before which caused such rage? "And having risen they threw Him outside the city, and led Him to a brow of the hill on which their city had been built, in order to throw Him down" (Luke 4:29—translation). This reveals the hatred religionists have for the Biblical doctrine of an election of grace (Rom. 11:5). The leper by the grace of the sovereign God had surpassed the religious training of Christ's enemies.

Unlike those who are the corrupt fruit of easy believism, the leper did not presume anything; but he learned experientially that he had been cleansed. He was not taught by Arminians on the basis of assumption to use the word "since," the first class condition which expresses reality—"Since you are willing, you can heal me." By grace he knew that the old sinful nature which had been born out of the source of the flesh continuously existed in him as sinful flesh. He said, "If you are willing, you are able to cleanse me" (Luke 5:12b—translation). And the Lord Jesus "...having extended His hand touched him saying: I am willing, you be cleansed at once; and immediately the leprosy departed from him" (Luke 5:13—translation). Hence, his physical cleansing demonstrated his spiritual cleansing on the basis of Christ's impending sacrifice with the same immediacy as his physical healing.

Following the leper's healing, Christ "...sternly charged and immediately sent him away, and says to him: See that you tell no one anything, but go show yourself to the priest and offer with reference to your cleansing the things which Moses commanded, for a testimony to them" (Mark 1:43, 44—translation). The things to be presented to the priest had the same relation to the cleansed leper as gladly receiving the word, baptism, and continuing steadfastly in the apostles' teaching had to the repentant Jews of Acts 2:38 or as baptism had to Paul (Acts 22:16).

The person who has been born out of God can testify that he has a spiritual nature existing in a continuous state as a spiritual nature: "and that which [*to*, definite article which agrees with the nominative neuter singular of the adjectival part of the participle of *gennao*, the subject of *estin*] has been born [perfect passive participle of *gennao*, completed action in past time with a resulting state of being] out of [*ek*, ablative of source] the Spirit [*tou*, ablative neuter singular agreeing with *pneumatos*, ablative neuter singular of *pneuma*, source] is [*estin*, present active indicative of *eimi*, to be or exist] spirit [*pneuma*, nominative neuter singular of *pneuma*, used as a predicate]" (John 3:6b—translation). By the use of the neuter gender, there should be no doubt that a person's nature is the point of emphasis. This may also be further illustrated by the neuter gender of "the holy thing"—"...for this reason also the holy thing [*to hagion*] being born [present passive participle nominative neuter singular of *gennao*] shall be called, Son of God" (Luke 1:35—translation). However, the only similarity between John 3:6b and Luke 1:35 is the neuter gender. The nature Christ assumed was impeccable, whereas the human nature of the Christian is peccable. The sex of a Greek substantive does not always correspond to that of an English substantive, because in Greek, gender is more a matter of grammar than sex. However, gender can be determined by the form of the word.

The Roman Catholics have a doctrine called "Immaculate Conception," which means Mary did not possess a depraved human nature because she was without the stain of original sin. On the contrary, Scripture proves that Mary rejoiced in God her Savior (Luke 1:46, 47). Their saying that Mary was conceived and born without spot or stain of original sin is a heretical, man-made doctrine. If Mary were absolutely free from original sin, why did she speak of the days of her purification (*katharismos*, cleansing or purification) (Luke 2:22)? Purification was needed for the parents of Jesus Christ, not for the child. Since sin is connected with mankind because of our solidarity with Adam in the fall, Jesus Christ cannot be related with the "new creation" in our need for purification, because He is eternally united with the Godhead. Sin can have no linkage with the God-Man except by its imputation to Him on behalf of the elect at Calvary.

Mary, like every other human being, was associated with John 3:6a—"that which has been born out of the flesh is flesh" (translation). Although having been born out of the Spirit, Mary, apart from the Holy Spirit coming upon (future middle indicative of *eperchomai*, to come upon, used 10 times— Luke 1:35; 11:22; 21:26, 35; Acts 1:8; 8:24; 13:40; 14:19; Eph. 2:7; James 5:1) her, could never have received, conceived, or brought forth the sinless Person who assumed human nature in her womb. As important as the virgin birth is to the Christian message, it does not completely explain the sinlessness of Jesus Christ. However, one must admit that the two truths are closely related. Even though our finite minds cannot fully comprehend the mystery of the incarnation (the hypostatic union of the Divine and human natures), we can lay hold of what we do not fully comprehend. This is the reason the statement "For with God nothing shall be impossible" (Luke 1:37) follows Luke 1:35.

The logic of the virgin birth, which means that Jesus Christ did not descend from Adam by ordinary generation, is recorded in Scripture. Therefore, the act of procreation (producing offspring) as such does not corrupt the offspring. At this point, let us give some thought to God's creation of Adam and Eve. From the formed (*yasar*, root meaning is form or fashion and is synonymous with create—God's creative activity) man of dust, God created Adam by breathing into him the breath of life; and from a rib of flesh, God created Eve. God creates as easily as He speaks. The human nature of Jesus Christ which He assumed in the incarnation was from the Father, through the Son, and by the Holy Spirit. Therefore, human initiation is completely excluded. This enables us to understand the total absence of sin from the Person and life of Jesus Christ. The Holy One came into personal contact with sin only by imputation at Calvary. On the cross, Jesus Christ vicariously and sacrificially bore sin on behalf of the elect. All the titles and designations the Son of God/the Son of man assumed indicate His identification with the elect as the subjects of Divine grace. Anyone blasphemes who says or thinks that Jesus Christ was identified with "fallen" mankind in either life or death except by imputation.

What God did in the womb of Mary, who had not only a nature having been born out of the flesh but also a spiritual nature having been born out of the Spirit, the person with

God-given faith believes; but he cannot comprehend it by reasoning. According to Luke 1:26-35, Mary had to be informed of the gift of grace. Furthermore, its significance was confusing to her, as it is to all the recipients of God's undeserved favor. Grace is not a reward for faith, but it produces faith. To miss the meaning of grace is to miss the total revelation of God to man. When Gabriel said to Mary, "Hail, thou that art highly favoured..." (Luke 1:28), he was not saying that she was a dispenser of grace but a recipient of God's undeserved favor. The Greek of Luke 1:28 reads, "...*chaire* [present active imperative second person singular of *chairo*, to rejoice or be glad], *kecharitomene* [perfect passive participle vocative feminine singular of *charitoo*, to favor highly]...." Translated it reads, "Rejoice, you have been highly favored...." Although Mary was endued with grace, she was not "full of grace" in the sense that Christ was full of grace (John 1:14-16). Mary was poor, yet rich; troubled, yet meditative; at first doubtful, but later believed (Luke 1:29, 38, 45).

Christians can relate with both having been born out of the flesh and having been born out of the Spirit (John 3:6). We know the continuing existence of our sinful human nature made no contribution to our having been born out of the Spirit. Furthermore, we know that although having been born out of the Spirit, we are not absolutely (completely, wholly, or fully) spiritual, but we were absolutely sinful before we were born from above. Having been born out of the Spirit, Christians have a new nature; however, we still have our old sinful nature, which by grace we are no longer under dominion. Birth from above, however, does not free one from having been permanently sold (perfect passive participle of *piprasko*, to be a slave to or sold under) under sin as to sin's penalty of physical death and the constant warfare between the Spirit and the flesh (Rom. 7:14, 25; Gal. 5:17). After all, why did the virgin, who brought Jesus Christ into the world as the God-Man, die? Furthermore, why was she troubled and doubtful, and thus, like us, in need of comfort and instruction?

Flesh alone satisfies flesh; spirit alone satisfies spirit (John 3:6). The more spiritual the worship by Christians, the less attractive it is to the flesh. The following is the order for worship: (1) Prayer is first in order because by the Spirit of adoption we cry, "Abba, Father" (Rom. 8:15). One who has been regenerated approaches God in prayer by the agency of the Holy Spirit within (Rom. 8:26, 27). (2) Worship is not in the realm of physical things (John 4:20-22). It is in the sphere of man's renewed spirit (I Cor. 2:11-15), bearing witness with God's truth. (3) Worship is the source of power for service (worship—Eph. 1-2, work—Eph. 3-4, and warfare—Eph. 5-6). The absence of worship signifies the absence of acceptable service.

The Lord Jesus contrasted true worshippers with false worshippers in His discourse with the woman of Samaria: "And the woman answered and said: I have no husband. Jesus says to her: you spoke correctly, I have no husband; for you have had five husbands, and he whom you now have is not your husband; this truly you have said. The woman says to Him: Sir, I perceive that you are a prophet. Our fathers worshipped in this mountain [Gerazim, where the Samaritans worshipped]; and you are saying that in Jerusalem is the place where it is necessary to be worshipping. Jesus says to her: Woman, believe me, for an hour is coming when you shall worship the Father neither in this mountain nor in Jerusalem. You are worshipping what you have not known, we worship what we have known, because salvation is of the Jews; but an hour is coming and it is now, when the true worshippers shall worship the Father in the sphere of the spirit and truth; for indeed the Father seeks the ones worshipping Him; God is spirit [a spiritual Being], and the ones worshipping Him must worship Him in the sphere of the renewed spirit and truth" (John 4:17-24—translation).

The Son came to seek and to save the lost (Luke 19:10). The Holy Spirit regenerates the ones for whom Christ died. The Father seeks worshippers. Worship signifies reverence, honor, and adoration. It agrees with Him who is worshipped. No one who disagrees with what God says worships Him no matter how sincere he is. Much that is called worship is not worship. One is incorrect to state that all religions have good in them. If all religions are right, the Bible does not mean what it says but what people think it says. The Holy Spirit alone can give the renewed person the knowledge of what is right or wrong. Therefore, we can know and embrace the Holy Spirit only with our spirits, an impossibility for the flesh. There is an initial renewal of one's spirit, and then there is a continuous renewal.

Worship is spiritual when the door of the new heart is closed to all intruders and open to the truth of God. Going into one's closet for prayer and closing the door is one thing, but the door of the heart left open while he supposes he is praying is another thing. Since God is Spirit, we must worship Him with our renewed spirits according to God's revealed truth. Two missionaries were ridiculed by a Catholic priest for ministering with only a Bible and a song book. However, there is no difference between the priest going from the Bible to altars, candles, crucifixes, etc., and the degeneracy of Christendom from God's word to Sunday School, Training union, bulletins, banners, dramas, gymnasiums, sports events, clowns, movies, musicals, family centers, etc. All these things are flesh feeding flesh. We worship only in our renewed spirits. We use our bodies in service; but we do not serve Jesus Christ in the sphere of the flesh but in the sphere of the renewed spirit.

God is spiritual in nature. He is nonmaterial substance of a pure unmixed essence and not limited by material substance or nature. A material body may be dissolved, but the Godhead is incapable of dissolution. The essence of God is indivisible and therefore cannot be divided into parts. The sun is entire in every place; shall not God who created the sun be much more than His created sun (Jer. 23:24; I Kings 8:27)? Since God is spirit, our approach to Him and our apprehension of Him must be spiritual in character. That which has been born out of the flesh can neither approach nor comprehend God. A spiritual nature is necessary to comprehend the truth concerning God; even then, we never fully comprehend Him. Believers are related with the spiritual order of things.

Natural thoughts of God may be degraded or elevated, but they tend to obscure what has been revealed. The Lord through Moses warned against degrading thoughts of God: "And the Lord commanded me at that time to teach you statutes and judgments, that ye might do them in the land whither ye go over to possess it. Take ye therefore good heed unto yourselves; for ye saw no manner of similitude [form] on the day that the Lord spake unto you in Horeb out of the midst of the fire: Lest ye corrupt yourselves, and make you a graven image, the similitude of any figure, the likeness of male or female, The likeness of any beast that is on the earth, the likeness of any winged fowl that flieth in the air, The likeness of any thing that creepeth on the ground, the likeness of any fish that is in the waters beneath the earth" (Deut. 4:14-18). The degradation of God by natural man is also magnified in Romans 1:23-32. The Lord through Moses also warned against thoughts that compare God with the elements He created: "And lest thou lift up thine eyes unto heaven, and when thou seest the sun, and the moon, and the stars, even all the host of heaven, shouldest be driven to worship them, and serve them, which the LORD thy God hath divided unto all nations under the whole heaven" (Deut. 4:19). We must neither degrade God by comparing Him with ourselves or creatures lower than ourselves nor elevate Him in our thinking to the sun, moon, stars, and elements above us. Either one obscures the revelation of God in Christ. We must beware of degradation and elevation. Men may speak highly of God, but everything must be brought to the test of Holy Scripture. The wicked may eclipse God's glory, but they cannot touch His essence.

God is spirit; therefore, He is omniscient (Ps. 139:7-10; Jer. 23:24). Since God is spirit, He can be comprehended only by the Holy Spirit. God is spirit; therefore, He can be worshipped only in spirit. Worship that is acceptable to God must be suited to His nature. Two kinds of worship, one of spirit and the other in truth, are not taught in John 4:24—"God is spirit, and the ones worshipping Him must worship Him in the sphere of the renewed spirit and truth" (translation). The preposition *en*, locative of sphere, indicates the sphere of the new nature and God's revealed truth. We must worship Him in the sphere of our new nature according to the revelation of the truth He has given to us. People who are heretical in their concept of God, Christ, salvation, etc., do not worship. One's spirit is not right if he is erroneous in what he believes. The renewed spirit is in opposition to external things, and the truth is in opposition to error. Hence, God cannot be worshipped in a renewed spirit and error. Spirit satisfies spirit, and flesh satisfies flesh. God is spirit, and the redeemed spirit of the believer is his highest excellence. Both the spirit of God and the spirit of man are mentioned in I Corinthians 2:11—"For who among men has known the things of a man except the spirit of a man in him? so also in the same way no one has known the things of God except the Spirit of God" (translation).

Since God is a pure spiritual Being, the following things are true:

1. God is a pure spiritual Being; otherwise, He could not be God the Creator. Every artificer first has his model in his mind. Man creates to the extent of forming a

mental image of something. Only in the externalization of his idea is man hemmed in. He is restricted by his finite nature.

2. God is a pure spiritual Being; otherwise, He could not be infinite in nature. He did not create at random. The act of a fool is to build without object. God did not create without a purpose.

3. God is pure spiritual Being; otherwise, He could not be one. "Hear, O Israel: the LORD our God is one LORD" (Deut. 6:4). If the pure spiritual Being possessed a body as a man, He would be capable of division. Where the greatest unity is, there is the greatest simplicity.

4. God is a pure spiritual Being; otherwise, He could not be invisible (I Tim. 1:17). Sometimes a representation of God but not of His essence is made to the inward sense. Sometimes men are said to see Him but only in the sense of fuller manifestation.

5. God is a pure spiritual Being; otherwise, He could not be independent. That which is made up of parts depends on parts, but God is not made up of parts. He is the eternal, indivisible One. The Triunity is not one plus one plus one, but one times one times one which equals one.

6. God is a pure spiritual Being; otherwise, He would not be immutable. "For I am the LORD, I change not..." (Mal. 3:6).

7. God is a pure spiritual Being; otherwise, He would not be omnipresent. "Know therefore this day, and consider it in thine heart, that the LORD he is God in heaven above, and upon the earth beneath: there is none else" (Deut. 4:39).

A body cannot be in two places at once. Wherever we are we know. A confusing thought to many is how bodily members can be ascribed to God. Since men are unable to conceive of a spiritual Being apart from physical attributes, these physical attributes as they bear some likeness to ours are used to signify the acts of God. God's wisdom is called His eye. His efficiency is represented by the arm. The sincerity of His affections is expressed by His heart. The revelation of His Divine will is called His mouth. The manifestation of His favor is portrayed as His face. Christ called Himself a vine, a branch, a light, etc. Who understands Him to literally be those things? God has assumed forms by which He has manifested Himself in the pillar of cloud, the burning bush, the elements, a more definite form, the fiery furnace as a man, and the angel of the covenant in the Old Testament. In the New Testament, He is the Son of man, God absolutely considered assuming and veiling Himself in human nature. It has been said that God is excellent without imperfection, a spirit without parts, great without quantity, perfect without quality, everywhere without place, powerful without members, understanding without ignorance, and highest who is infinitely beyond.

Man's inability to see what he was never intended to see is no imperfection in his nature. Man was never intended to see God absolutely considered with his physical eyes. God is invisible. A spirit can be known only by its operations through a material body. Hence, God manifested Himself not to sense but to experience. God has revealed Himself in the humanity of the Lord Jesus. He is the image of the invisible God (Col. 1:15). How absurd and abominable are all other images, pictures, etc. Can we make an image of that which we have never seen? No man has seen God. Since God is everywhere present, it is absurd to worship Him by an image. We are not to use the ceremonies of the Old Testament, like the tabernacle, priesthood, and offerings, because Jesus Christ has come; and He is the fulfillment of all those types and shadows. Since we are not to use the ceremonies which God once appointed, should we use things He never appointed? He never appointed anything but the word of God for us to use to study and worship Him in the sphere of the renewed spirit according to His truth. There are two parts in worship but not two kinds of worship.

God's attitude toward His people who do not follow His precepts is jealousy. "For the LORD thy God is a consuming fire, even a jealous God" (Deut. 4:24). (See Ex. 20:5; 34:14; Deut. 4:24; 5:9; 6:15; 32:16, 21; Josh. 24:19; Ezek. 16:38, 42; I Cor. 10:22.) I Corinthians 10:22 shows that the principle in the Old Testament is carried into the New Testament. The existence of jealousy in God implies the existence of love. Jealousy in God is never spoken of except in reference to those He loves. He is jealous of His people. God has a right to our love because He has shed abroad His love in our hearts. Any wandering of affection and any deviation of allegiance carries wounds and provocation to jealousy. Do we as God's people seek pleasure in the company of His enemies? "Adulteresses, have you not known that the friendship of the world is hatred toward God? Therefore whoever may desire to be a friend of the world, is being constituted an enemy of God" (James 4:4—translation). "For they [Israelites] provoked him to anger with their high places, and moved him to jealousy with their graven images" (Ps. 78:58). "Little children, keep yourselves from idols..." (I John 5:21). An idol is anything which comes between the believer and the Lord.

Jealousy is the shadow cast by love. The greater the love the greater the shadow. All sin is a characterization of virtue, and sin never looks so shameful as when placed beside the virtue it characterizes. As a musician revolts against a discord, the soul rich in love revolts against whatever impinges on and violates that love. Jealousy, like anger, can be either good or bad. We are to be angry at sin without sinning (Eph. 4:26).

Lack of anger at sin manifests that one does not love the Savior. Jealousy is evil when it is against the joy or success of another and when it is suspicious of another without foundation. In such cases, it can be the rage of a man (Prov. 6:34). Nothing can satisfy such rage. Wrath is cruel, and anger is outrageous. But who is able to stand before envy? Elijah's jealousy for the glory of God and His truth was good: "...I have been very jealous for the LORD God of hosts: for the children of Israel have forsaken thy covenant, thrown down thine altars, and slain thy prophets with the sword; and I, even I only, am left; and they seek my life, to take it away" (I Kings 19:10). Paul applied the same principle stated by Elijah to the Corinthians: "I wish you would be patient with me in a little foolishness; but indeed you are being patient. For I am jealous over you with a godly jealousy, for I have betrothed you to one husband that I might present you as a pure virgin to Christ" (II Cor. 11:1, 2—translation). Paul's jealousy was not envy that the Corinthians were following other teachers, but he was anxious over them lest being led astray by false teachers they might be deceived.

Jealousy is the anger and pain of injured and insulted love. God cannot remain silent when He loses any of the affection, trust, or reverence by which He has stirred our souls. Jealousy is sensitive awareness to any abatement or transference of affection.

In concluding the study of John 3:6, the following things should be evident to every sincere believer:

1. That which has been born out of sinful nature will never in time be anything but sinful nature (John 3:6a).

2. That which has been born of the Spirit shall exist forever as a spiritual nature (John 3:6b).

6

NECESSITY FOR REGENERATION

> Do not wonder because I said to you: It is neces-
> sary for all of you to be born from above. The
> Spirit is breathing where He desires, and you are
> hearing His voice, but you have not understood
> where He is coming from and where He is going;
> thus is everyone who has been born out of the
> Spirit. —John 3:7-8 (translation)

There are only three basic views of the new birth: (1)
pelagian—what I must do to be saved; (2) concurrent—man
cooperates with God to bring about the new birth; (3) free
grace—the Scriptural teaching experienced by every child of
God that salvation is all of God. Christ did not teach doing
and leaving undone. His was the principle of being and
becoming. The new work is created before it can be lived.
Hence, the child of God goes from positional sanctification
by the grace of God to progressive sanctification in which the
recipients of grace become more like Him.

In contrast to Christ showing Nicodemus his responsibility

and stating the general nature of that responsibility, Christ had been speaking to Nicodemus about the new birth. He did not, as some assume, speak of an entire change of nature. Nothing recorded in John 3:1-8 hints at Jesus Christ changing the nature of the sinner. The old nature is not changed (v. 6). Regeneration is not the changing of the old nature, but it is the impartation of a Godlike nature. The Lord gave us the principle of spiritual life in the new birth; and by the power of this spiritual life, He enables us to overcome the old nature that remains in us. There is a continual warfare between the old and new natures in every person who has been saved by the grace of God.

Christ's statement in John 3:7—"Do not wonder because I said to you: It is necessary for all of you to be born from above" (translation)—does not mean what most people think. The verb *dei*, meaning must or necessary, is usually represented as man's duty. However, man has no more to do with birth from above than he does with his physical birth. Every physical birth produces a life that did not previously exist except in purpose. Furthermore, birth out of the Spirit is a person's coming into existence as a Christian who did not exist as a Christian before, except in God's eternal covenant of grace. Birth from above is supernatural, instantaneous, invisible, and eternal. No place in Scripture is "born of God" ever presented as man's duty. The imperative mood is never associated with the work which is exclusively God's.

Confusion about the subjects of God's sovereignty and man's birth from above is evidenced by people who say, "The sinner must invite Jesus into his heart," and "Open the door of your heart and let Jesus in." These statements are unscriptural, but they are not as absurd as the statement made about Christ's discourse with Nicodemus by persons who give lip service to God's sovereignty in regeneration: "Do not wait to think about the new birth until you understand it, as

Nicodemus did, or you may never experience it." What is the basic difference between the first statements and the last? The first statements are made by people who believe that sinners are active in their birth from above. The last statement is declared by persons who talk about God taking the initiative in regeneration, but they then refute their declaration in their discussion of it. Those who categorically deny that God takes the initiative in regeneration do not differ from those who first admit it, but within the context of discussing regeneration, they deny it. The latter deserve greater ridicule because they talk out of both sides of their mouths.

Many in professing Christendom think they were born Christians because their parents were Christians. A woman once came to an inquiry room where a noted evangelist asked her if she was a Christian. She replied in the affirmative. When asked the length of time she had been a Christian, she said she was born one. The preacher congratulated her on being the first he had ever met who was born a Christian, because all others were born children of Adam. A Christian was asked by his professor where he was born, and he replied by giving the names of two cities. The interrogator questioned how he could be born in two different cities. The Christian answered by quoting John 3:10—"...Art thou a master of Israel, and knowest not these things?" The Christian had been born out of the flesh in one city, and he had been born out of the Spirit in the second city. One having been born from above has been born a Christian.

Christ said to Nicodemus, "Do not wonder because I said to you: It is necessary for all of you to be born from above" (John 3:7—translation). The negative adverb *me* used with the aorist active subjunctive verb *thaumadzo* becomes a prohibition; therefore, it is used like a present imperative. The cause of the prohibition is significant because of the meaning of the impersonal verb *dei* and the use of the second person plural pronoun *humas*, you. The translation of the Greek words *dei humas gennethenai anothen* is "It is necessary for all of you to be born from above." "It is necessary" is the translation of the present active indicative of *dei*. It does not refer to man's duty but to God's purpose. Will any attempt to say that God is unjust to determine to regenerate some when He would have been just to determine to destroy all? All of God's chosen ones from among both Jews and non-Jews (John 10:16) will be born from above, thus constituting one flock with one Shepherd. "...and as many as have been appointed [*tetagmenoi*, perfect passive participle nominative masculine plural of *tasso*, to appoint or designate] to eternal life believed" (Acts 13:48—translation). Hence, God's purpose determined that the elect shall believe, and His purpose shall be accomplished: "...My purpose will be established, And I will accomplish all My good pleasure" (Is. 46:10 NASB). (Study Eph. 1; Rom. 8; John 10; 17.) Furthermore, the pronoun *humas*, accusative masculine plural of the pronoun *su*, meaning you, proves that Christ had more in mind than the one to whom He was speaking. Not only is it a necessity for the elect to be born from above, but it is also determined by God that they shall be made alive in Jesus Christ.

The Lord Jesus Christ closed His discourse on the necessity of being born out of God by showing how sovereignly and mysteriously it is accomplished: "The Spirit is breathing where He desires, and you are hearing His voice, but you have not understood where He is coming from and where He is going; thus is everyone who has been born out of the Spirit" (John 3:8—translation). Since commentators are divided on whether the word *pneuma* should be translated wind or Spirit in John 3:8, Biblical evidence should be considered.

The Greek word *pneuma* is used 363 times in the New Testament, and most of the references designate the third

Person in the Godhead. He is given such titles as the Holy Spirit (Matt. 28:19), Spirit of God (Rom. 8:9), Spirit of Christ (Rom. 8:9), Spirit of truth (John 14:17), Spirit of life (Rom. 8:2), Spirit of adoption (Rom. 8:15), Spirit of grace (Heb. 10:29), etc. The noun is also used when speaking of the nonmaterial part of man (Acts 7:59; I Cor. 5:5), the inner perceptive part of man (I Cor. 2:11), demonic spirits (I Tim. 4:1), angels as ministering spirits (Heb. 1:14), the spirit of the Lord Jesus (John 19:30; Rom. 1:4), etc. Although the noun *pneuma* is neuter gender in the Greek, it is translated correctly in Scripture as "He" or "Him" when the demonstrative masculine pronominal adjective *ekeinos*, he, is used (John 14:26; 16:8, 13, 14) and also in other references where the adjective is not used, such as Romans 8:16, because He is a Person. Gender to the Greeks was a matter of syntax rather than sex. Since the Holy Spirit is a Person, we should speak of His Person as He or Him and not it.

The word *pneuma* is translated "wind" only in John 3:8 in a number of English translations; but without any reservation, this author believes that translation is incorrect for the following reasons: (1) The immediate context opposes the translation of *pneuma* as wind. Christ was not giving an analogy of comparison, as some believe, but He was explaining as much as we can understand about the mysterious work of the sovereign Spirit in regeneration (John 3:5-7). (2) As God breathed physical life into man formed of dust from the ground (Gen. 2:7), the Holy Spirit breathes spiritual life in the ones He desires (John 3:8). (3) It seems unlikely that Christ would use an analogy that does not have the ability to move and choose at its own discretion. Recognizing that there are no perfect analogies in created matter to illustrate spiritual achievements, an impersonal wind blowing where it desires runs amuck without the control of the sovereign God Himself. This is to say nothing about the meteorological explanation of air movements and speed controlled by high pressure and low pressure areas. Since we are not making a study of meteorology, all we need to understand is that the sovereign God controls the wind movements. (4) Some use the adverb *houtos*, which is translated "so" in many English translations, as proof that our Lord was making a comparison. The adverb *houtos* can be used thus—in the same way, like this, thus, or so. The adverb "thus," meaning in the way indicated, is used in our Lord's declaration, "The Spirit is breathing where He desires, and you are hearing His voice, but you have not understood where He is coming from and where He is going; thus [in the way indicated by what Jesus Christ had said] is everyone who has been born out of the Spirit" (John 3:8— translation).

Heaven is a prepared place for a people purposed by God in eternity. Christ's work on the cross in time was God's provision for accomplishing His purpose. The application of the provision by the Holy Spirit to the passive elected sinner is the beginning of spiritual life in the lost sheep. According to our context, the person who has been born out of a corrupted physical nature cannot, because of his depraved condition, make any contribution to his being born out of the Spirit. Furthermore, regeneration is not the result of the Spirit's use of means. The light of day was not a means of restoring sight to the blind man. Physical food is a means of physical growth, but it presupposes physical vitality. Likewise, the word of God is a means to spiritual growth, but it presupposes spiritual life. No desire for the word exists in spiritually dead persons. The new life is not implanted because man perceives the truth of God, but he perceives the truth on account of life that has been implanted.

God's purpose does not begin when one first understands truth. Many speak of preparatives for regeneration, but those who refer to people seeking, knocking, and praying ignore the fact that what they call preparatives for regeneration are, if they are genuine, the manifestations of regeneration. Whatever conviction is wrought in a person before regeneration is nothing more than conviction of conscience; it is not of one's will. Some Reformers are not without error concerning preparatives for regeneration. The preaching of the law or the gospel to bring about conviction cannot be said to be preparation for being born from above. To know that one is a sinner and deserves hell is not preparation for the regenerating work of the Holy Spirit. Some are of the opinion that the enlightening work of the Spirit precedes His illuminating work in regeneration. This is unscriptural, and persons who have heard the truth preached must be warned against the idea that they are obligating God to regenerate them. Regeneration is not an act of debt but of grace.

Regeneration is the beginning of spiritual existence, but not the beginning of physical existence. Regeneration is God's work; conversion is man's turning to God in the power of the regenerating Holy Spirit. Conversion occurs with the newly implanted nature. Regeneration is a single act, complete in itself, and never repeated. Conversion is the beginning of a holy life which manifests itself by a series of constant and progressive holy acts.

SECTION II

THE OBJECTIVE ASPECT OF LIFE
John 3:9-15

7

THE OBJECTIVE REVELATION OF CHRIST

Nicodemus responded and said to Him: How can these things come into being? Jesus replied and said to him: You are the teacher of Israel and you have no knowledge of these things? Truly truly I am telling you, we are speaking what we have known and are testifying what we have seen, and you are not receiving our witness. Since I told you earthly things and you are not believing, how shall you believe if I may tell you heavenly things? And no man has ascended into heaven except the One having descended from heaven, the Son of man. —John 3:9-13 (translation)

Having completed His discourse on the subjective work of the sovereign Holy Spirit in regeneration, Christ turned to the objective revelation of Himself. In answer to the third question by the teacher of Israel, "How can these things come into being?" (translation), Christ replied, "You are the teacher of Israel and you have no knowledge of these things?" (John 3:10—translation). Arminians step in at this point to talk about Nicodemus' traditional preoccupation. Those who believe in gospel regeneration say that since men are regenerated by the preaching of the gospel, Nicodemus at this point had not been given the gospel. Those who teach baptismal regeneration believe every birth has three stages in the ultimate change in regeneration: (1) the planting of the seed, (2) the gestation period, and (3) the delivery. They believe the seed is the word of God planted in the sinner's heart. Their opinion is that the Holy Spirit operates through the word which is living and active. Their idea is that the gestation period comes subsequent to the planting of the seed. They assume that, meeting the conditions of faith and repentance, the sinner is brought to life by the Spirit who not only has arranged the meeting of the sinner and the preacher, but also gives life at the time of baptism. In contrast to these beliefs, Nicodemus was without the subjective work of grace by which he could hear and understand what Christ was teaching.

Nicodemus' problem was that he was not hearing Christ's voice, because the Holy Spirit had not breathed life into him (John 3:8). The word for "voice" is *phone*, voice or language. Christ used this same word when He said, "To this One the doorkeeper opens, and the sheep hear His voice [*phone*], and He calls [*phonei*, present active indicative of *phoneo*, to call, call forth, or summon] His own sheep by name and leads them out" (John 10:3—translation). The following are characteristics of regenerated sheep: (1) They recognize the voice of the Shepherd (John 10:3). (2) They believe His teaching (John 17:8). (3) They have spiritual discernment (I Cor. 2:12; Heb. 5:14). (4) They have the mind of Christ (I Cor. 2:16). (5) They try the spirits (I John 4:1). (6) They follow the Shepherd (John 10:4). (7) They flee from false shepherds (John 10:5).

Some say Nicodemus had been led by Jesus Christ into a psychological attitude of teachability. Their argument is based on what they describe as a change of attitude between the questions of John 3:4 and the question of John 3:9. In a day when religionists have substituted psychology for the Holy Spirit and their humanistic appeals for the word of God, no wonder they would make such a statement about Nicodemus. Sinners are being told that they must have self-esteem because of their importance as somebody. Preachers who tell people what they want to hear become successful in the eyes of men. In religious revival campaigns, people are told, "the Lord has done all He can, and now the result is left to you." One's depraved ego is inflated to think his destiny is left to his decision. Religious excitement, great crowds, and many decisions are no criterion for spiritual awakening.

Living in an age when religionists have been influenced by the same psychological training given to business men, politicians, athletes, etc., concerning the secret to success, some uninformed believers are being affected by a reprogramming of the mind. Christians are subjected to the same reprogramming in the work place. Since the subconscious mind is said to be stronger than the conscious mind, the stimulus operating below the threshold of consciousness as a result of the reprogramming will cause uninformed Christians to suggest things that do not identify with the spiritual realm. In order for people to be successful in the work place, they are taught the following things: (1) Self-confidence—you are able, or you can do this job. (2) Self-image—You must have a good picture of yourself. (3) Success motivation—Your desire must be stronger than your fear. (4) Enthusiasm—You must think that nothing is impossible for you in this job. (5) Creativity—You must have imagination in order to be creative. (6) Winner's attitude—There is no such thing as being a good loser. (7) Stop procrastinating—Do not put off until tomorrow what you should do today. (8) Effective communication—Learn to communicate well with fellow workers. (9) Decision making—Learn to make decisions on your own. (10) Personal dynamics—Be driven by the force of your religious faith.

Every informed Christian has no problem knowing that some of these things do not relate to the Christian life. Promoters of these rules in the work place usually introduce them by making such statements as, change your mind and you change your course; you will have a wonderful life if you feel good about yourself; you are as good as anyone else, because God made you good.

Following Christ's statement to Nicodemus, "You are the teacher of Israel and you have no knowledge of these things?" (translation), He began to give the objective truth concerning Himself, which the unregenerate religious teacher was not receiving. "Truly truly I am telling you, we are speaking what we have known [perfect active indicative first person plural of *oida*, to know, understand, or perceive] and are testifying what we have seen [perfect active indicative first person plural of *horao*, to see, experience, or understand], and you are not receiving [present active indicative of *lambano*, to receive] our witness" (John 3:11—translation). The two perfect tense verbs demonstrate the positive message of Christ based on His present knowledge founded on His past experience. Christianity is a positive message, because its foundation is the positive Being of God. Since man is a positive sinner admitting no question, before he can receive the positive unquestionable message of the gospel, he must have the positive breath of life breathed into him. When this takes place, he will receive the word for himself, thus experiencing a conversion which cannot be questioned.

To further establish the fact that Nicodemus had not been regenerated, Christ said, "Since [first class condition which affirms reality] I told you earthly things and you are not believing, how shall you believe if [*ean*] I may tell [*eipo*, aorist active subjunctive of *lego* with *ean*, third class condition, is more probably future condition] you heavenly things?" (John 3:12—translation). Preachers who think they can make the Scriptures relevant (suitable or fitting) to the unregenerate are forced to admit, whether they believe it or not, they have exchanged the word of God for their own depraved opinions. (See Rom. 1:25.) Whatever is relevant to the unregenerate is not relative to Holy Scripture, and whatever is suitable to the Scriptures is not relative to the unregenerate (John 3:19-21; I Cor. 2:14). Any person who thinks he can make spiritual things suitable to the natural man understands neither man's depraved condition nor the spirituality of heavenly things. Apart from being born from above, one is possessed by the only nature he has, the one born out of the flesh. His heart is ruled by his depraved nature, and he is a slave to the passions of his corrupt heart.

The revelation of God in the Son of man is the heart of the gospel: "And no man has ascended into heaven except the One having descended from heaven, the Son of man" (John 3:13—translation). Some manuscripts add, *ho on en to ourano*—"who is in heaven." The Son of God assumed the human nature provided Him by the Father into such personal union that He is properly called either the Son of God or the Son of man. Thus, we have a Savior who preexisted as the Son of God and became the one Mediator of God and of men, the man Christ Jesus who gave Himself as a ransom for all of God's elect (I Tim. 2:5, 6a).

Christianity involves a change which may be compared to a birth from above. That birth is accomplished by the work of the sovereign Spirit. However, it could never be accomplished by the Spirit apart from the eternal Son of God becoming the Son of man in one Mediator of God and of men for the purpose of becoming a ransom for the sheep. In speaking about the subjective work of Christianity, Christ mentioned only the initial act of being born from above. In speaking of the cause of the subjective work, the Lord Jesus introduced His objective work on the cross. Therefore, the

distinguished from "live" in order to look (Ezek. 16:6). God does not bring His people into what His love purposed to give us without first teaching us what the flesh is and will always be in its corrupt nature. Spiritual life is in the risen and glorified Christ because of His sacrificial death at Calvary.

The type we are considering in Numbers 21 teaches that sinful flesh has been condemned, and condemned flesh will never be changed (Rom. 8:3). Life involves the gift of the Holy Spirit; and by the power of the Spirit, the regenerated person must put to death the deeds of the body (Rom. 8:10, 13). This is accomplished by looking to the One symbolized by the serpent of brass. Hence, the remedy provided in the death of Jesus Christ heals the repentant and believing sinner as many times as needed (I John 1:7).

Having introduced the subject of John 3:14-15, taken from the type of Numbers 21, contextual evidence must first be considered in the relationship of the serpent of brass to Israel before it is typically applied to the subject of conversion in John 3. Actually, Numbers is the "Book of the Wilderness," because it describes the experiences of Israel in the wilderness. This seems to be the better title since the book covers Israel's wanderings and experiences in the wilderness. Therefore, it is the book of order, service, failure, and victory. Since service is impossible without order, God described in great detail the order for Israel's pilgrimage (Num. 1-4). The truth that order is heaven's first law is portrayed in the first ten chapters of Numbers: (1) A census was taken to determine every person's pedigree (Num. 1). (2) The order of the Israelites for their physical welfare was given (Num. 2). (3) The order of the Levites, the spiritual leaders, was given for Israel's spiritual welfare (Num. 3). (4) A Divinely ordered system, assigning to each man his work so that there were no gaps, was given (Num. 4). (5) The Israelites must be separated from defilement (Num. 5). (6) The Israelites were taught separation and humiliation, and benediction was pronounced on them for their separation and humility (Num. 6). (7) The tabernacle was dedicated for worship (Num. 7). (8) The Levites, the spiritual leaders, were consecrated (Num. 8). (9) The guiding cloud of shekinah glory appeared (Num. 9). (10) The trumpets were sounded to call the people to the assembly meeting (Num. 10). No failure that has happened or may happen should be allowed to hinder Christians from seeking the Divine order.

The book of Numbers assumes that the Israelites had knowledge of their redemption, the covenant, and their identification with the tabernacle. These three subjects are fully discussed in the book of Exodus. Subsequent to the completion of the tabernacle (Ex. 40), all the instructions given in the book of Leviticus (regulation of access to God) were given within a period of one month to prepare the Israelites for their wilderness journey (Ex. 40:17; Num. 1:1). None except those who could declare their pedigree were numbered for identification with the tabernacle. The entire life of Israel was built around the tabernacle. Likewise, the whole life of Christians should be built around the assembly. The tabernacle typifies not only the place of worship but also the place from which we serve the Lord. All the movements of Israel in the wilderness were considered in association with the tabernacle, because she knew what it meant to be identified with the tabernacle. These principles are to be applied by Christians to the assemblies of Christ. No service separate from a local assembly is acceptable to God. Christians are not unattached units with liberty to do as we please.

Since Numbers is the book which narrates the history of the Israelites in their testing and preparation for entrance into Canaan, it covers Israel's history from the completion of the law-giving at Sinai to the borders of Canaan. The book of Numbers should be contemplated in its relation to the first three books of the Bible—Genesis, Exodus, and Leviticus. This scrutiny will lead one from created man's fall and depravity in Genesis, to his redemption by blood at the passover and deliverance by power at the Red Sea in Exodus, to access to God in worship and laws that regulate that access in Leviticus, and then to service and provision for that service in Numbers.

This book of service records five great types of Jesus Christ as the Son of man to supply the need of His people on earth in our pilgrimage: (1) The manna portrayed provision for physical sustenance (Num. 11:7-9). (2) The red heifer offering typified provision for daily sins of the flesh (Num. 19:1-10). (3) The water from the rock foreshadowed provision of the priesthood (Num. 20:7-11). (4) The serpent of brass symbolized provision for revealing the nature of sin and its remedy (Num. 21:1-9). (5) The Star of Jacob prefigured provision for hope during Israel's wilderness pilgrimage (Num. 24).

FIRST—The first type of Christ as the Son of man to supply the need of His people during our pilgrimage on earth was the manna for Israel's physical sustenance, which portrayed Jesus Christ as the bread of life for the sustenance of His people (Num. 11:7-9; John 6:31-35). The Israelites had many distractions from without and from within in their pilgrimage to Canaan. From without they were pursued by Pharaoh and intercepted by Amalek. From within they had a mixed multitude, and many of the Israelites themselves listening to the mixed multitude murmured. The hangers-on are usually the originators of most problems in the assemblies of Christ. Discontented people have no problem finding the discontented; therefore, they will join in quarreling with God's provisions. Wickedness never plays a negative game. When persons start complaining against God, they will soon show hostility against His will. "And the mixed multitude that was among them fell a lusting [had greedy desires—NASB]:

and the children of Israel also wept again, and said, Who shall give us flesh to eat?" (Num. 11:4). There is nothing so damaging to the spiritual growth of God's people as their association with people of mixed principles. From murmuring to lusting and from lusting to the tearful expression of extreme vexation is a terrible downgrade.

Israel's turpitude is a reminder that the nature born out of the flesh is flesh. That means flesh in Christians is no better than flesh in the unregenerate. Thus, the Israelites began to crave the same things as the mixed multitude. Furthermore, their weeping was not over their sins but because they could not have what they desired. Surely we have not forgotten the spirit of discontent concerning the order of God's house that invaded the assemblies in Jerusalem and Corinth (Acts 6; I Cor.). Human orders which rob some believers of spiritual joy and privilege continue to prevail in Christendom.

Complaining is a sign of ingratitude. Israel could see nothing other than she had no flesh to eat. Murmuring is always one-sided; therefore, the Israelites saw only the lights, not the shadows of Egypt. Their thoughts turned to the absence of flesh to eat, and they were not thankful for the manna, God's provision for their need. They did not rely on God's promise to supply their every need: "And my God will supply fully your every need according to His riches in glory in Christ Jesus" (Phil. 4:19—translation).

Although Israel complained many times between Exodus 14 and the completion of God's law at the close of Leviticus, the kind of judgment we read about in Numbers 11:1-3 was not executed. The Israelites were new converts at their first complaining. During the time between their first and second complaints about no water, they had received much instruction and had received God's leadership according to the truth to which they had been exposed. But now a great distance separated them from the point in time of their first complaining. What was the difference between then and this point in Israel's sojourn? The answer is twofold: (1) She had promised to obey the law which God had spoken through Moses, but she soon forgot that pledge when God put her to the test. (2) She had been given good instructions for her physical and spiritual good in addition to the promises which should have motivated her. God reminded her of how He had borne her on eagles' wings and brought her to Himself (Ex. 19:4). There were no conditions to what the sovereign God had done for Israel, as there are no conditions to our being born from above. However, God requires things of those who have been born from above. Israel had not only been taught more than when she first left Egypt, but she had also promised to obey what God commanded. Her promise to obey was soon forgotten when she felt her flesh was being neglected. This angered God, and He consumed the Israelites with fire until Moses interceded on their behalf. The place where they were consumed was named Taberah in order to perpetuate the memory of the peoples' sin. Every Christian in every age is under the moral law of God. New Testament applications of judgment are made on the children of God who know the truth but fail to obey it. They will be chastened and some are killed (I Cor. 11:30; I John 5:16).

"Evangelicals" commit the same sin as the murmuring Israelites when they desire license to sin rather than God's will. When they are confronted with Christian responsibility to obey Christ's commands, they cry, "legalism," or "grace killers." In contrast to their definition of legalism, the Bible defines legalism as the result of people taking what God has commanded His people to do for their conditional spiritual benefit and making those commands necessary for one's deliverance from the penalty of sin. God's law given to Israel was never meant to be a means of positional deliverance, but it was given as a result of such deliverance. Doing what one loves to do is not legalism. Christ said to His disciples: "If you may love Me, you shall keep My commandments" (John 14:15—translation). The Psalmist proclaimed his love for God's commandments: "O how love I thy law! it is my meditation all the day. Thou through thy commandments hast made me wiser than mine enemies: for they are ever with me. I have more understanding than all my teachers: for thy testimonies are my meditation. I understand more than the ancients, because I keep thy precepts. I have refrained my feet from every evil way, that I might keep thy word. I have not departed from thy judgments: for thou hast taught me. How sweet are thy words unto my taste! yea, sweeter than honey to my mouth! Through thy precepts I get understanding: therefore I hate every false way" (Ps. 119:97-104). The Biblical teaching of progressive sanctification is not "rely and relax" but "trust and obey." The antinomian erroneously claims that the believer has no more to do with the moral law than a citizen of one country has to do with the law of another country.

SECOND—The second type of Christ as the Son of man to supply the need of His people in our pilgrimage on earth was the red heifer offering, which typified Jesus Christ as the provision for our daily sins of the flesh (Num. 19:1-10). This offering is not mentioned among the offerings when the tent of meeting was first instituted (Num. 19:1-22). Since the wilderness was the place where the true character of the flesh manifested itself, the red heifer offering was God's provision for the wilderness. If Christians will consider how the flesh manifested itself in Numbers 11-16, we will understand the moral necessity for the true Israel of God being purified from her uncleanness. Her flesh desired human guidance, murmured, lusted, preferred Egypt's food, and rebelled against Divine authority. Believers cannot say that we have never come into moral contact with what Paul calls "the body of this death" (Rom. 7:24). The things of the flesh demonstrated by the Israelites in their wilderness journey exhibit themselves in our lives as Christians. As God provided the red heifer offering for Israel's sins of the flesh, He has made provision in the offering of Jesus Christ for the sins of the flesh in Christians. When believers allow fleshly motives and desires to work in our lives, we have touched that which is dead. Death is the seal of the Divine curse. The same old problem that evidenced itself in the redeemed Jews manifests itself in the saints of God today. How can we pamper the flesh when we see it condemned in the sacrifice of Jesus Christ (Rom. 8:3)?

Aaron did nothing in connection with the red heifer. Eleazer (his name means "God is helper"), who was a type of the saints, was associated with the red heifer offering. This typified the need of saints in our wilderness experience. The red heifer being offered only once portrayed that Jesus Christ by the sacrifice of Himself brought about a permanent purification of all the sins of the elect as far as our position in Christ is concerned. Nothing can affect our position. But our condition can be affected by our sinning so that we lose fellowship. Our position is stationary, but our condition fluctuates. Since the Levitical system was incompetent to accomplish permanent purification, all the offerings of that system were required to fully describe the one perfect sacrifice offered once for all. In the one Person of Christ is found the essential truth that He who fully revealed God fully redeemed the elect of God. As the elect's Substitute, the judicial claim against us has been removed by the satisfaction of Divine justice in the Person of the Father's eternal Son. (See Heb. 9:12-14; 10:10-14.)

The essential difference between the red heifer offering, which stood for the whole house of Israel, and the other sacrifices was that once offered it did not need repeating by the Israelites. It was for a redeemed people. Its virtue remained, because the ashes were the memorial of an accepted sacrifice(Num. 19:9, 10, 17, 21). A female rather than a male was used in this offering, because the redeemed of God are referred to in the feminine gender—wife in the Old Testament and spouse or bride in the New Testament. The ashes represent the power of a completed sacrifice. The running water (living water, not blood) represents the Spirit of Christ cleansing the unclean Christian. Both the unclean and the clean persons, the one who has been contaminated by the dead and the clean person who sprinkled the water on the unclean, shall cleanse themselves. The closer to Christ believers get, the more we are affected with a sense of our uncleanness. The new nature cannot rise to new heights without the Christian mortifying the deeds of his old nature. Purifying is not optional; it is for all of God's people (II Cor. 7:1). Therefore, the priest (not Aaron) should take cedar wood, hyssop, and scarlet, and cast them into the midst of the burning of the heifer as an expression of nature from its highest elevation to its lowest depth (Num. 19:6). (See Is. 2:12-17; Phil. 3:3-11.)

THIRD—The third type of Christ as the Son of man to supply the need of His people in our pilgrimage on earth foreshadowed the provision of the priesthood (Num. 20:7-11). This truth is portrayed in our Lord's statement to Moses at Israel's second experience of having no water: "and the LORD spoke to Moses, saying, Take the rod; and you and your brother Aaron assemble the congregation and speak to the rock before their eyes, that it may yield its water..." (Num. 20:7, 8 NASB). The wilderness was the place where the true character of the flesh came into full view. Israel was at the end of her wilderness journey, but her flesh was unchanged, which harmonizes with what Christ said to Nicodemus, "That which has been born out of the flesh is flesh..." (John 3:6a— translation). The second generation of Jews committing the same sins as the first, as soon as they left Egypt by the power of God through the Red Sea (Ex. 17:7), proves that we learn little or nothing from history.

This second test of no water was to bring out the provision and value of the priesthood of Jesus Christ typified by Aaron. Priesthood in this aspect of truth supposes infirmities on the part of the Israelites. There was no need in this instance for smiting the rock as at Israel's first Meribah experience (Ex. 17:6, 7). Since the efficacy of the smitten rock abides, only speaking to the rock was necessary. The fulfillment of these types is explained by Christ Himself in John 10 and John 17, by Paul in Romans 8:28-34, and by the writer of Hebrews in Hebrews 7 and Hebrews 10. Priesthood is viewed completely in its resurrection form.

God's people stumbling within a few steps of the goal is indeed sad, but that is what Moses did when he disobeyed God by speaking unadvisedly to Israel and then striking the rock twice rather than speaking to it (Num. 20:9-11; Ps. 106:32, 33). Admittedly, Moses had been exposed to some trying circumstances with Israel. At the first Meribah test, Israel criticized Moses because she had no water. The people overlooked the fact that God had brought them to this place (Ex. 17). However, the peoples' outrage against Moses did not bring retaliation from Israel's leader at that point in his ministry. He took their complaint to the Lord: "...What shall I do unto this people? they be almost ready to stone me?" (Ex. 17:4). Moses was sharing the same trial with the people. In addition, he had the responsibility of leading them. Moses may have followed the example of our Savior and asked for which of his good works were they stoning him (John 10:32). Although Moses was a meek man (Num. 12:3), his besetting sin was sensitivity and a quick temper (Ex. 2:12). Therefore, at the second Meribah experience, Moses lost his temper and said, "Listen now, you rebels; shall we bring forth water for you out of this rock? Then Moses lifted up his hand and struck the rock twice with his rod; and water came forth abundantly, and the congregation and their beasts drank. But the LORD said to Moses and Aaron, Because you have not believed Me, to treat Me as holy in the sight of the sons of Israel, therefore you shall not bring this assembly into the land which I have given them" (Num. 20:10-12 NASB). This had nothing to do with their position, but it did involve their condition. The first generation of Jews failed under Moses; the second generation failed under Joshua; are we failing under Christ?

FOURTH—The fourth type of Christ as the Son of man to supply the need of His people in our pilgrimage on earth was the serpent of brass, which symbolized the provision for revealing the nature of sin in God's people and its remedy (Num. 21:1-9). The Savior applied this type in John 3:14-15. No apology for the historical territory covered thus far is appropriate, because it is necessary to build a case that is absolutely irrefutable in the light of the immediate and overall contexts of Scripture. Christ was not telling Nicodemus what he had to do to be born from above, neither did He quote a passage from the Old Testament that told a redeemed and delivered people how they could be born from above.

The interpretation generally given of John 3:14-15 is that Christ likened Nicodemus to the dying Israelite whose look of faith at the brazen serpent brought health and life (Num. 21:1-9). Those who thus interpret these verses believe that as soon as the consciously guilty sinner entrusts himself to the crucified Savior, the Holy Spirit operates the miracle of the new birth, and the life then received is eternal. Conversely, John 3:14-15 does not tell what a passive sinner must do to be born from above. Conversion and regeneration do not come in the same manner. Regeneration is the act of God the Holy Spirit on the passive sinner by which He imparts the principle of life. Conversion is the act of the regenerated sinner by the power of the indwelling Spirit of life to embrace Jesus Christ as Lord through the gospel message. This is the initial conversion experience, and many other conversions will follow in the Christian life.

Adam's descendants have been infected with the serpent's venom so as to be called a generation of snakes (Matt. 3:7). Original sin does not lose its fermentation in the redeemed. By trials alone the redeemed learn experientially that the nature of sin never changes for the better and that sin which brought the sentence of death on all men is very much alive in all men, even in the elect who have been delivered from its penalty. Sin is not abolished in those who have been born from above, but it has been condemned (Rom. 8:3). Christians know that the principle of sin in them has been condemned, and they also know they have the last word in the dramatic dialogue with death. "But now having been made known by the coming of our Savior Christ Jesus, on one hand having canceled death on the other hand having brought life and immortality to light by means of the gospel" (II Tim. 1:10—translation).

The serpent of brass foreshadowed Jesus Christ as He was lifted up on the cross. As the serpent was a reminder of the curse, the cross on which Christ Jesus suffered reminds the elect that there He became a curse on our behalf (Gal. 3:13). God condemned sin on the crucified One at the cross. Sin's heinous nature came by man, and deliverance from its guilt and consequences must also come by Man who is more than man, Jesus Christ the God-Man. The Kinsman Redeemer is the nearest relative any person can have. (Study the book of Ruth.) The serpent symbolized the curse caused by sin, and the brass typified God's judgment falling on the One made a sin offering. Therefore, deliverance was experienced by the redeemed Israelites' looking at the objective serpent of brass lifted up on a pole (Num. 21), and deliverance is experienced by regenerated sinners' looking at the objective Savior lifted up on the cross. Further consideration of what has taken place in our lives will reveal that apart from the subjective life, the objective experience would have been impossible.

Numbers 21 clearly reveals that at this point in Israel's history the people were characterized by overcoming their enemies. Their enemies represent fleshly principles which are opposed to that which is spiritual in the people of God. God never purposed to bring His people into what His love desires until we have learned the fight we must wage in order to gain the spiritual height that pleases Him. Surely we have not forgotten the song "Higher Ground." Spiritual life is in the risen Savior; therefore, it is altogether outside the life of flesh, because believers live in the sphere of resurrection since we have been raised by God's grace (Col. 3:1). The bite of the serpent is the Divine conviction of what the flesh truly is in the source of its being. God's design is to bring His people to judge the root of our problem, the principle of sin that remains in us subsequent to our regeneration and conversion.

Numbers 21:1-3 is a good introduction to what follows in verses 4-9 concerning the serpent of brass. Israel's victory over Arad (the name means "wild ass of trading") was soon forgotten. No one would deny that the king of material prosperity has taken many captives. As warriors for Christ, we must never become so entangled in the affairs of life that we cease to be good soldiers (II Tim. 2:4). After knowing the deliverance and faithfulness of God for many years, we know the sin principle remains in us; and we are not at liberty to do what the flesh desires. Therefore, the battle intensifies rather than diminishes with growth.

Israel's journey from mount Hor to Edom caused her to be discouraged because of the way (Num. 21:4). Because of our newly found joy, Christians are prone to overlook trials. However, before long the honeymoon experience is over, and we find that the Christian life is no parade on a level road that is protected from trials. The wilderness through which we travel is often very difficult on the flesh. Although there is nothing in the wilderness to nourish the spiritual life, we enjoy spiritual blessings while we are in it. The hostility and warfare we encounter on the way become very trying, but God's grace enables us to stand against evil forces. The battle is often personal hand to hand combat; thus, we do not come out without wounds. (See Eph. 6:10-18.) One of the most discouraging things about warfare is the avoidance of conflict by some. Paul knew what it was to have comrades to let him down (II Tim. 4:16). The discouraged Israelites' speaking against God and Moses caused God to send fiery serpents among the people, which caused many of the people to die a physical death. The repentant looked and lived; the unrepentant died. This same tragedy came to some of the Corinthians (I Cor. 11:30). Thus, their condition but not their position in Christ was affected.

Following the judgment of the fiery serpents, the Israelites came into conditions that were common with the "land of the well." The water came not from the rock, but from the well which rose up from within the Israelites. (See John 4:14.) The well had been choked with ignorance, discouragement, and complaint. God's judgment had killed some and caused others to repent and be converted by looking at the serpent of brass. Divine things must be known by experience before they govern our lives. Therefore, Christian experience precedes Christian practice. When the fountain has been purified, the stream is pure; therefore, the Christian life is represented not by a stagnant pool but by living, running water. Grace not only conquers but it also fights. The converted Israelites were now living in the joy and power of the ascending well. It was then that Israel sang, because they had discovered the Rock following them; and that Rock was Christ. (See I Cor. 10:1-11.)

The events of Numbers 21:7-35 are great spiritual landmarks which must not be ignored:

1. Israel's conversion (vv. 7-9) came by her looking at the

serpent of brass, because she had already been delivered by blood and by power (Ex. 12; 14).

2. Israel journeyed toward the sunrising (vv. 10-16) because her conversion led her in the right direction, since it pointed to God's purpose. (See Josh. 1:15; 13:5.)

3. Israel's conflicts were now the wars of the Lord (vv. 11-14).

4. Israel's song came from inward satisfaction (v. 17). Here is the subjective experience of the Holy Spirit's expressing Himself in testimony.

5. Israel sought to pass through enemy territory peaceably (v. 22; 20:17). Today's literature, social prestige, political influence, and professing Christendom are all against the true assemblies of Christ. Therefore, we have no form of government, civil or ecclesiastical, to impose on the nations of the world. If our worship is affected, we must obey God rather than man.

6. Israel defended herself, but she was not the aggressor (vv. 23-32).

7. Israel was victorious because God delivered her enemy into her hand (vv. 33-35).

The only other reference in the Old Testament to the brazen serpent is II Kings 18:4. That which had been designed for a good purpose became a great evil. The brazen serpent had not been mentioned for nearly 800 years. Hezekiah, the seventh good king of Judah, set out immediately to restore what Ahaz, his wicked father, had destroyed. Although Hezekiah's father was wicked by precept and example and supported all kinds of heathen customs, he left behind a good son. Hezekiah has been called a Jewish Iconoclast—a person who attacks cherished beliefs and traditional customs which are based on error or superstition, or a breaker or destroyer of images. Among the many things Hezekiah destroyed was the brazen serpent made by Moses. He called it "Nehushtan," which means a piece of brass. The King saw a lifeless senseless piece of brass in what the people accounted as a god and to which they burned incense. The brazen serpent was never intended to be an object of worship. It was an object lesson pointing to something greater. Every symbol loses its significance and true value if it is converted into an idol.

The brazen serpent suggests to us the danger of going beyond the Divine command in what some term religious duty. God commanded the serpent to be made and used, but there is no record that He commanded its preservation, as He did in the case of the golden pot that contained the manna, Aaron's rod, and the tables of the covenant. This emphasizes the importance of Christian observances and duties being fulfilled according to God's word rather than according to peoples' superstitious ideas. Failure to maintain what God has set forth to be observed in His assemblies is just as erroneous.

King Hezekiah manifested fearless honesty when he called the brazen serpent "Nehushtan," a piece of brass. His boldness was possible because "He trusted in the LORD God of Israel; so that after him was none like him among all the kings of Judah, nor any that were before him. For he clave to the LORD, and departed not from following him, but kept his commandments, which the LORD commanded Moses. And the LORD was with him; and he prospered whithersoever he went forth..." (II Kings 18:5-7). Things should be called by their correct names; therefore, no man of God should ever low-key idolatry, heresy, or wickedness. Calling things today by their proper names is a rare virtue.

FIFTH—The fifth type of Christ as the Son of man to supply the need of His people in our pilgrimage on earth was the Star of Jacob, which prefigured provision for our hope (Num. 24:15-19). The "Star out of Jacob" was a prophecy given by Balaam, the one who has been called a strange mixture of a man. Three chapters are devoted to the description of this incredible man (Num. 22-24). Balaam, whose name means "confounding the people", was a man who was not only gifted with natural abilities, but he also had some knowledge of God. Unregenerate people can have a natural knowledge of some basic Biblical principles. Some people are disturbed over God having spoken to Balaam (Num. 22:9, 12, 20; 23:4), putting a word in his mouth (Num. 23:5, 16), and the spirit of God having come upon him (Num. 24:2). But this is not disturbing seeing that "the LORD opened the mouth of the ass, and she said to Balaam, What have I done unto thee, that thou hast smitten me these three times?" (Num. 22:28). Balaam's prophecy resembles that of Caiaphas: "Nor consider that it is expedient for us, that one man should die for the people, and that the whole nation perish not. And this spake he not of himself: but being high priest that year, he prophesied that Jesus should die for that nation; And not for that nation only, but that also he should gather in one the children of God that were scattered abroad" (John 11:50-52).

At this point in Numbers 22-24, the Spirit had turned aside from the history and experience of Israel in the wilderness to discuss the strategies of her enemies. One would think that subsequent to the serpent of brass in Israel's history, she would have learned to judge the flesh, give place to the Spirit, and be victorious over influences which are hostile to God. However, God must now make known to His people that hostile counsels against Him were in progress. Although there was no open warfare, secret plans to curse Israel were in the making. Can Satan succeed to curse the people of God and thus prevent their entering the promised land? The question now was neither deliverance from Egypt nor conversion but progressive sanctification. Satan works overtime and uses newly devised schemes to try to keep God's people from entering their promised possessions. Hence, as soon as God's people learn about the weakness of the flesh and God's remedy for it, Satan changes his tactics. He tries to curse what God has blessed, which is impossible because God's people have been elected, redeemed, and positionally set apart in Jesus Christ. (See Rom. 8:29-39.)

Balaam had some knowledge of God, but with him was an unholy mixture of good statements with wicked actions. The following are some of his good statements: "If Balak would give me his house full of silver and gold, I cannot go beyond the word of the LORD my God, to do less or more" (Num. 22:18). "How shall I curse, whom God hath not cursed? or how shall I defy, whom the LORD hath not defied?" (Num. 23:8). "...Let me die the death of the righteous, and let my last end be like his" (Num. 23:10). Some of Balaam's evil actions were the following: "Balaam smote the ass, to turn her into the way" (Num. 22:23). "And Balak [waster] said unto him, Come, I pray thee, with me unto another place, from whence thou mayest see them: thou shalt see but the utmost part of them, and shalt not see them all: and curse me them from thence. And he brought him into the field of Zophim, to the top of Pisgah, and built seven altars, and offered a bullock and a ram on every altar" (Num. 23:13, 14). Like Balaam, a price is attached to the sermons of some eloquent preachers who put all their religion in their discourses and all their pathos in their voices. Peter said that Balaam loved the wages of unrighteousness (II Pet. 2:15). A better perspective of Balaam is gained by learning of Balaam's counsel (Num. 31:8, 16; Micah 6:5), soothsaying (Josh. 13:22), curse (Josh. 24:9, 10; Neh. 13:2), way (II Pet. 2:15), error (Jude 11), and doctrine (Rev. 2:14). Balaam was one of the ten persons named in Scripture who said, "I have sinned." Only five of them turned from sin: David (II Sam. 12:13), Nehemiah (Neh. 1:6), Job (Job 7:20), Micah (Micah 7:9), and the prodigal (Luke 15:18). These are the five who did not turn from sin: Pharaoh (Ex. 9:27), Balaam (Num. 22:34), Achan (Josh. 7:20), Saul (I Sam. 15:24), and Judas (Matt. 27:4).

Four prophecies are attributed to Balaam in Numbers 23-24, but the one we are concerned about in connection with our subject is his last recorded prophecy in Numbers 24:15-25. "I shall see him, but not now: I shall behold him, but not nigh: there shall come a Star out of Jacob, and a Sceptre shall rise out of Israel, and shall smite the corners of Moab, and destroy all the children of Sheth" (Num. 24:17). Like Caiaphas, Balaam made some true statements. Jacob and Israel were mentioned in all of Balaam's prophecies. In his first prophecy, Balaam raised the question, "How shall I curse, whom God hath not cursed?" (Num. 23:8). The second prophecy revealed that Balaam could not revoke the blessing God had bestowed on Israel, or the reason for it: "...he hath blessed; and I cannot reverse it. He hath not beheld iniquity in Jacob, neither hath he seen perverseness in Israel..." (Num. 23:20, 21). This prophecy points to Israel's position through blood redemption. However, in God's dealings with her from the standpoint of her condition, the Lord noticed everything. Balaam's third prophecy revealed a freshness which pleased the Lord that could not be dried up. Finally, Balaam saw a Star that should come out of Jacob whose authority will destroy all of Israel's enemies, and He shall reign.

9

OBJECTIVE LIFE REALIZED

And just as Moses lifted up the serpent in the desert, in like manner it is necessary for the Son of man to be lifted up. —John 3:14 (translation)

The foundation of the gospel message was stated by Jesus Christ in John 3:14. Christ's message originated in God's eternal covenant of grace (Heb. 13:20); therefore, from God's perspective, the One speaking to Nicodemus was "the Lamb who was slain [perfect passive participle of *sphadzo*, to put to death or slay] from the foundation of the universe" (Rev. 13:8—translation). Furthermore, He was the One "having been foreordained [perfect passive participle of *proginosko*, to know beforehand or to foreordain] on the one hand before the foundation of the universe" (I Pet. 1:20—translation). Now, this One in time soon would be lifted up on the cross on behalf of all the ones included in God's covenant of grace, because He is the One having descended out of heaven for that purpose (John 3:13).

Subsequent to Christ's resurrection, He asked the two men

on the road to Emmaus, "Was it not necessary [*ouchi*, the emphatic form of the adverb *ou* which is used interrogatively; in addition, an imperfect active indicative of *dei*] for the Christ to suffer these things and to enter into His glory?" (Luke 24:26—translation). There was necessity but not compulsion in Christ's death: "For this reason the Father loves Me because I lay down My life, in order that I may take it again. No one took it from Me; on the contrary I lay it down from Myself. I have authority to lay it down, and I have authority to take it again; I received this commandment from My Father" (John 10:17, 18—translation). God was not bound absolutely but conditionally to give His Son to die, because His death supposes the entrance of sin and the only way the guilt of sin could be settled. Although there was no necessity on God's part for sin to enter the human race, His wisdom decreed that it should enter for the purpose of His own glory. God created man mutable with the possibility of sinning for the reason that the immutable God cannot create immutability. Whatever God creates must of necessity be inferior to the Creator. Therefore, man was created mutable; but he was not created sinful, as man born out of sinful nature is sinful. Man, not God, is the author of his own sinful nature.

The affirmation that evil in the world of mankind is inevitable will pose a problem for many unless they are willing to consider this fact in the light of the supreme Sovereign of the universe. God's purpose to order things in such a way that evil should come into existence in mutable mankind for the fulfillment of His eternal purpose is no argument that He does not hate evil as evil. Transgression against God demands no less than death, because sin against the infinite God is infinite crime. Therefore, punishment must be infinite in order to be equal to the crime. Punishment equal to the crime is justice, but punishment less than the crime is injustice. Since God was not obligated to prevent the fall of man, neither was He obligated to redeem man after the fall. However, in order to redeem those the Father chose from among sinful men, the Son of God out of necessity must die in order to provide an infinite sacrifice. However, His death was not mandatory by an antecedent compulsion, because God would have been just had He punished all eternally (infinitely).

The term "necessity" indicates that God out of His good pleasure having elected some to be redeemed, regenerated, converted, progressively sanctified, and glorified was under obligation to accomplish this fivefold deliverance through the sacrifice of His Son. As the Father was free from any obligation, from the standpoint of order, until the forming of the eternal covenant of grace, the Son was not obligated to die, and the Holy Spirit was not compelled to apply what the Father had purposed and the Son purchased. The covenant of grace made mandatory the lifting up of the Son for the elect and the breathing of life into them by the Holy Spirit. Justice is characteristic of all three Persons in the Godhead. The eternal covenant of grace was a unilateral covenant in which the three Persons in the Godhead were in perfect agreement. It excluded man who could have no place in the fellowship of equals in such a work.

The analogy Jesus Christ used in His discourse with Nicodemus must not be overlooked in its use in either the life of Israel in her wilderness journey or its relationship to the subject of regeneration in John 3. As the uplifted serpent of brass had nothing to do with God's deliverance of Israel from Egypt, believing in the uplifted Christ has nothing to do with God's regenerating a passive sinner. Although an analogy is a partial similarity between like features of two things, one does not have the liberty to allow his imagination to run wild and go beyond the contexts of each feature when making a comparison. Israel's deliverance by blood in Egypt was not by her looking at the uplifted serpent of brass. Furthermore, the regenerated sinner is not born from above by believing in

Jesus Christ. He believes in Jesus Christ as a result of his having been born out of God.

Everyone who believes the truth concerning the death of Jesus Christ for the sins of the elect is interested in what the Son of God has done on behalf of those who believe. One's believing does not enable him to attain the spiritual life provided for him, but his God-given faith enables him to experience the life Christ provided for him at Calvary. Attaining (to succeed in reaching or gaining something) and experiencing (to learn from experience what one has) life differ. Therefore, the subjective spiritual life causes the regenerated person to hunger and thirst for objective spiritual life, which is experienced by believing the objective message concerning the Person and Work of Jesus Christ. Spiritual life must be imparted in the passive sinner before he can experience the objective life of Christ's work at Calvary.

Being born from above and believing in Christ are completely different aspects of eternal life: (1) Regeneration is subjective; conversion is objective. (2) Regeneration is righteousness imparted in God's elect; conversion is belief by the regenerated one in imputed righteousness. (3) Regeneration is actual apart from the person's consciousness of it; conversion is his conscious experience of believing in judicial righteousness. Being born from out of the Spirit is life in the subjective sense. Faith in Christ is life in the objective sense.

This is the most common but unscriptural statement made today: "The sin of unbelief is the only hindrance to one's salvation." Unbelief is caused by the sin of depravity. Unbelief, although a negative word, is positive. It issues from a positive cause. Thus, the direct cause of one's unbelief is his own depraved will. Furthermore, if he is not one of Christ's sheep, he will never believe; thus proving that the experience of salvation is not left to the ability of depraved people to determine whether or not Christ shall have any objects of love. People are not believing because they are not Christ's sheep: "You are not believing, because you are not from My sheep" (John 10:26—translation). Some Arminians have manifested spiritual ignorance by saying that the meaning of this verse would be simpler if the clauses were reversed. But a reversal would change the meaning to, "You are not from my sheep, because you are not believing." This heresy is self-evident to the Christian, because he knows that his spiritual birth has been out of God rather than out of his faith. There is no difference between reversing the clauses of John 10:26 and reversing the Biblical order of regeneration by the sovereign Spirit and conversion by the regenerated person's believing in Jesus Christ as He is presented in the gospel (John 3:1-15). A reversal would destroy both regeneration and conversion.

Scripture teaches that Christ's sheep for whom He died were crucified with Him. In giving his testimony to the Galatians Paul said, "I have been crucified with [*sunestauromai*, perfect passive indicative of *sustauroo*, to be crucified together, to crucify with another, or to be crucified with another in a spiritual resemblance] Christ [*Christo*, instrumental of *Christos*]; and I am no longer [*ouketi*] living [present active indicative of *dzao*], but Christ is living [present active indicative of *dzao*] in me; and the life that I am now living [present active indicative of *dzao*] in the sphere of the flesh, I am living [present active indicative of *dzao*] by [*en*, instrumental of means] the faith from [*pistei*, ablative of source of *pistis*] the Son of God who has loved [aorist active participle of *agapao*] me and has given [aorist active participle of *paradidomi*] Himself on behalf of [*huper*] me" (Gal. 2:20—translation). The perfect tense of the verb *sustauroo* renders the translation, "I am crucified," in the King James Bible incorrect. It should be translated "I have been crucified," point action past time with a continuing state of result. The perfect tense signifies that Paul had been permanently crucified with Christ. The passive voice is used because neither Paul nor any other of God's elect were present when Christ was crucified. Nevertheless, we can say with Paul, "I have been crucified with Christ." The indicative mood of this verb signifies the reality of our crucifixion with Christ. Although one may use the objective genitive instead of the ablative of source to translate the "faith," the truth that faith comes from God is not destroyed. Faith is the gift of God. This verse teaches the same principles we have been investigating in John 3.

Consider the things taught in Galatians 2:20—

1. There are three paradoxes in this verse.

   (1) Judicial paradox—"I have been crucified with Christ." In this paradox, the cross came between Christ and Saul of Tarsus. To make a personal application, the cross came between God and me. How could Paul have been crucified with Christ when he was not present at the time when Christ was crucified? He was among the elect who were legally redeemed in the penalty paid by Christ at Calvary. This portrays a Biblical principle. Christ's death at Calvary was accomplished on behalf of all of those the Father had given to Him in the covenant of redemption.

   (2) Spiritual paradox—"I am no longer living, but Christ is living in me." In this paradox, the cross came between Saul and his sinful nature. Make it personal. The cross comes between me and my sinful nature.

   (3) Practical paradox—"the life that I am now living in the sphere of the flesh I am living by the faith from

the Son of God." In this paradox, the cross came between the world and Saul of Tarsus. Personally, the cross comes between the world and me. I am living by the faith God has given to me through the redemptive work of Jesus Christ.

2. Three crosses are taught in this verse.

   (1) The external cross is connected with the judicial paradox. It is outside of oneself.

   (2) The internal cross is united with the spiritual paradox. This is the subjective work of the Holy Spirit in the individual.

   (3) The practical paradox is joined with the cross which every Christian must take up and bear.

3. The three divisions of this text portray the central theme of Romans 6-8.

   (1) The judicial paradox is portrayed in Romans 6.

   (2) The spiritual paradox is revealed in Romans 7.

   (3) The practical paradox is described in Romans 8.

Some of the important things in this passage of Scripture may be considered from another point of view. The following three truths are included in our being crucified with Christ: (1) Christ was crucified. (2) We have been crucified. (3) We have been crucified together with Christ. The Lord Jesus died; we died; and we died together with Christ. This does not imply any fellowship with Christ in the act of mediation in the sense of being crucified in our own persons. We were not present. Christ paid the penalty, and the elect were spared. Legally, we have been forgiven. In dying in our place as our Surety, Christ did not stand as a private but a public Person.

He, the spotless, absolutely holy Lamb of God, was our representative at the cross. He was there on our behalf. The benefits purchased by Jesus Christ were made ours as though we had been crucified in our own persons. Thus, we are made partakers of the blessings of Christ (I Pet. 2:24; II Pet. 1:1-4).

Christ did not go to the cross in His own name but in the names of the elect. He was crucified for us, that is, on behalf of the elect of God. As Adam's act of sin in Eden in effect was also ours, Christ's act of obedience at Calvary in effect was also ours apart from any guilt in Him as our Substitute. He was there bearing our sins which had been imputed to Him. As all mankind had a death in sin in Adam, the elect had a death to sin in Jesus Christ. Adam was a type of Jesus Christ as a representative man. He represented all mankind, and Christ represented all the elect among mankind. (Read Rom. 5:12-21.)

The perfect passive indicative of *sustauroo*, crucified, proves that this crucifixion guaranteed Paul's actual dying to sin at some subsequent time. Its legality was taken care of in the death of Jesus Christ. That which took place at Calvary nearly 2,000 years ago guaranteed the regeneration and conversion experience of the elect. Subsequent to our crucifixion at Calvary, we were actually made dead to sin by regeneration. We knew nothing about it until in the power of the Holy Spirit we embraced the Lord Jesus Christ and had a glorious conversion experience. This means Jesus Christ is the life of the believer. He purchased our redemption, and that redemption purchased at Calvary was applied to us when the Holy Spirit breathed life into us.

So far as the claims of justice are concerned, all the Old Testament saints were made alive on credit (Rom. 3:24-26). They could be saved on credit because Jesus Christ the eternal Son was destined to go to Calvary, and nothing could prevent

His accomplishing what the Father purposed Him to do. Hence, what had been judicially imputed to Paul at Calvary became a reality to him in regeneration and conversion. Saul had died to the law's condemnation because his Substitute, Jesus Christ, had satisfied every demand of the holy law. So far as the claims of justice are concerned, all the elect were crucified with Christ. Therefore, identification with Christ at Calvary means the elect have satisfied the law in Christ by rendering obedience that is demanded, suffering its curse, and being released from its penalty.

The elect were not literally crucified with Christ, but the visible crucifixion of Christ at Calvary was a sign of our spiritual crucifixion which He suffered. Therefore, that which legally satisfied the holy God is effected in the elect at God's appointed time. There is a time to be born, a time to be born again, and a time to die.

Concerning death, some important things in their proper order should be considered:

1. Before the creation of the universe, Jesus Christ was foreordained to die. In God's eternal purpose, this presupposed man's death in the garden of Eden.

2. Jesus Christ actually died at Calvary for the elect (John 19:30).

3. All who were ordained to believe died with Christ at Calvary (Acts 13:48).

4. The legal death accomplished by Christ at Calvary is applied at God's appointed time to each one for whom Christ died (John 3:8). Thus, one is made a new creature in Christ by being born from above.

5. Christians are constantly experiencing a twofold death: (1) "always carrying about in the body the dying of Jesus, in order that the life also of Jesus may be manifested in our body" (II Cor. 4:10—translation); and (2) Christians are commanded, "You put to death therefore the members on the earth, fornication, uncleanness, passions, evil desire, and covetousness which is idolatry" (Col. 3:5—translation).

6. There is a final act of dying. Paul as a Christian said, "For me to be living is Christ and to die is gain" (Phil. 1:21—translation). Death to the Christian is nothing more than walking through its shadow, because both the sting of death, which is sin, and the victory of the grave have been canceled. The final act of dying brings the final change. As we received a body from God suited for life on earth, Christians at death shall receive a body suited for the heavenly kingdom. Although death is an alarming subject for most people, for the Christian it is the final change for glory.

Contrary to what religionists teach, regeneration is not effected by faith. It is effected in the elect by the Spirit in regeneration which produces faith. Life in the believer does not mean he was the agent of that life, but he is the subject. Life is neither self-derived nor self-maintained. God-given life is maintained by the grace that God gives and by the living faith we have in Jesus Christ. The new life is not less active than the old. Where there is spiritual life, there is spiritual activity. Thus, the life believers live in the sphere of the flesh is by a principle implanted in us by the Spirit of regeneration. In other words, this spiritual life is life within a life. Physical life is life in the sphere of the flesh; but while living in the sphere of the flesh, the Christian has spiritual life. Although we live in the flesh, we do not live after the flesh. Therefore, the spiritual life in us may be said to overrule the natural life in us for higher and nobler purposes. This is Christianity. God gives us life in order that this spiritual life can control the inferior life, the life in the flesh. Such life can never come to a standstill, because Christ works in us to will and to do of His good pleasure (Phil. 2:12, 13). We live as members in the Head, Jesus Christ.

Saul, the self-righteous Pharisee, died; Paul, the apostle, was living; but the ego remained. Nevertheless, Paul's life was no longer self-centered but Christ-centered. Anyone who by grace possesses eternal life is no longer self-centered. He is Christ-centered.

The following are examples showing that the Christian life is full of paradoxes: (1) Christian existence is a death and yet a life (I Cor. 15:31; II Cor. 4:16). (2) The believer lives and yet he is dying (II Cor. 4:10). (3) The believer's life is a life in the flesh, but not according to the flesh (I Pet. 1:14).

The old life of Saul the Pharisee, which is descriptive of every unregenerate person, may be explained as follows: (1) His law was self-interest. (2) His inspiration was self-love. (3) His goal was self-satisfaction.

On the other hand, the life of Paul the apostle, which is descriptive of every regenerate person, may be explained as follows: (1) His law was the interest of Christ. (2) His inspiration was the love of God, that love which was shed abroad in his heart by the Holy Spirit. (3) His goal was the glory of God.

Christian living in the sphere of the flesh is not easy, but the life itself is immortal. Religionists, because they are super-optimistic, do not want to talk about the hardships of the Christian life. However, Paul was not super-optimistic. Consider his suffering: bad eyes (Gal. 4:15), weakness, fear, and much trembling (I Cor. 2:1-5), the thorn in the flesh (II Cor. 12:7-10), persecution on the outside (II Cor.

11:12-15), persecution from weak brethren on the inside (I and II Cor.), and forsakenness by his own comrades in the faith (II Tim. 4).

The Christian life is immortal. The sun may say every morning, "I am come that the earth may have light, fields may grow, vineyards may be fruitful, and the landscape may be filled with joy." The sun may add, "I am the resurrection; I raised the buried seas from their graves. However, these earthly plants shall perish." On the other hand, when the Son of God said, "I am come that they might have life, and that they might have it more abundantly" (John 10:10) and "I am the resurrection and the life..." (John 11:25), there was an added dimension of importance. That dimension refers to the recipients of grace who have eternal life and shall never perish. Unlike the plant that begins to decay when it stops growing, the life that Christ gives the elect makes everlasting progress in knowledge, usefulness, and glory. Thus, the Christian life goes from strength to strength, grace to grace, and glory to glory. Spiritually, the believer is a changed person not when he believes but before he believed, because faith is the fruit of the change.

The Greek construction in Galatians 2:20 is not the same as it is in verse 16. In Galatians 2:16, faith refers to the faithfulness of Jesus Christ. Whereas in Galatians 2:20, faith refers to the life we are now living by faith which has come from the Son of God. It is His gift to us. Faith is a grace by which we believe God the Father, Jesus Christ, the Holy Spirit, and the word He has given us. In this God-given faith is (1) assent—faith is acquiescing; (2) consent—faith is agreeing; and (3) trust—faith is trusting, confiding, and relying in God-given faith. Christians live by faith, but life precedes the operation of faith. This faith is the fruit of life.

SECTION III

RESULTS OF SUBJECTIVE
AND OBJECTIVE LIFE
John 3:16-21

10

ETERNAL LIFE FOR THOSE GOD LOVES

> For in this way God loved the world, so that He gave the unique Son, in order that everyone believing because of Him may not perish but may have eternal life. —John 3:16 (translation)

The conjunction "for" (*gar*) in this verse, John 3:16, points back to what had been said. The words "in this way" (*houtos*, an adverb) point to what follows. This adverb is connected with God "loved" (aorist active indicative of *agapao*). It explains God's love. The verb *agapao* is used in the constative sense. It views the verb in its entirety. When did God the Father begin His love for the elect? God's love did not have a beginning. It is eternal: "...I have loved thee with an everlasting love: therefore with lovingkindness have I drawn thee" (Jer. 31:3). We love Him because He first loved us. God has always loved those He chose in Christ Jesus. Conclusively, the adverb *houtos* must be understood in the light of the verb it amplifies.

How should we view the love of God? He loved the world

(*kosmos*). Should we think of God's love as being so extensive and so intense that He gave His unique Son? Does the word *kosmos* include everyone without exception? Most people think this refers to the extent of God's love. However, this text does not refer to quantity but quality. It speaks of the depth of God's love, the character of that love. The word *kosmos* can be used many ways. For instance, it is used three times in John 1:10 and has a different meaning each time: "He [Christ] was in the world [*kosmos*, inhabited world], and the world [*kosmos*, material world] was made through Him, and the world [*kosmos*, world of unbelievers] did not recognize Him" (translation).

The word *kosmos* in II Corinthians 5:18-19 refers to those the Father gave to the Son in the covenant of redemption: "And all things from God the One having reconciled us to Himself through Christ and having given to us the ministry of reconciliation, as that God was in Christ reconciling the world [*kosmos*, the world of the elect] to Himself..." (translation). Everyone without exception will not be reconciled to Jesus Christ. Only those the Father gave to the Son, without the loss of one, will be reconciled. Jesus Christ was sent from the Father because He loved us eternally. He came down to where we were. The Holy Spirit imparted in us the work Jesus Christ accomplished at Calvary, and the love of God was poured out in our hearts. As a result, Christians love one another. This love is expressed by all its recipients, and it goes back up in praise, honor, and glory to the One who loved us with eternal love. Thus, the constative use of the verb *agapao* in John 3:16 contemplates love in its entirety.

God loved the world "so that [*hoste*, a superordinating conjunction introducing a dependent clause describing result] He gave [aorist active indicative of *didomi*, which means gave; this is another constative verb which views the action in its entirety]..." (translation). God cannot love us apart from

the death of His Son who became our Substitu¹
in Christ; therefore, the death of Christ is just
the Father as His love. That is why we are tol¹
13:8 that His blood was shed in the mind and
before the foundation of the universe. Hence, the depth and
character of His love is based on the death of Jesus Christ.

God gave "the unique [*monogenes*, only or unique] Son."
There is none equal with Him. There has never been and will
never be one like Him. He stands alone in quality. He is the
embodiment of unique characteristics. Jesus Christ walked on
the earth as the God-Man who alone is the Substitute for those
chosen by the Father. God gave "the unique Son, in order that
[purpose clause] everyone [*pas*] believing [present active
participle of *pisteuo*] because of [*eis*, accusative of cause]
Him may not perish [aorist middle subjunctive of *apollumi*]
but [*alla*, the strongest adversative in Greek] may have eternal
[*aionios*, accusative direct object] life" (translation).

No Christian has the authority to tell a lost person that God
loves him and Christ died for him. The book of Acts records
all the missionary journeys of the apostles, the establishment
of many local assemblies, and Peter's famous sermon on the
day of Pentecost. Not once in the entire book is anything said
about God loving you and Christ dying for you. No servant
of Christ told people that God loves them. Paul did not carry
a placard saying, "smile God loves you." All the servants were
doing what God commanded. They were sheep hunting, and
that is all we are commanded to do. To tell a lost sinner that
God loves him is failure to distinguish between the ones God
loves and the ones He hates. God does not love everybody:
"...Jacob have I loved, but Esau have I hated" (Rom. 9:13).

John 3:16 must be contemplated in the light of its context,
since *gar* points to the preceding verses and *houtos* points to
the verses following. According to the context of John 3:16,

here is no appreciation for God's love in the hearts of unregenerate people. To tell people who love darkness rather than light that God loves them is like casting pearls before swine. "Do not give that which is holy to the dogs, nor throw your pearls before the hogs, lest they shall trample them with their feet and having been turned may attack you" (Matt. 7:6—translation). This does not mean that a lost sheep may not act like a hog or a dog. An example is the apostle Paul who acted like a hog and attacked people before the grace of God came into his heart and life. The lesson is one of reverence for the truth of God and discretion in witnessing and in admitting persons into the assembly fellowship.

Following the subject of lawful judgment in Matthew 7:1-5, Christ showed the importance of exercising discernment pertaining to false prophets who come in sheep's clothing when they are actually wolves seeking to destroy with their false doctrine. Christians must be capable of making proper discrimination between dogs or hogs and sheep. Paul warned the Philippian saints about false professors by using three imperatives of *blepo* in Philippians 3:2—"You beware of dogs, beware of evil workmen, beware of false circumcision" (translation). (Study Rom. 2:28, 29; Gal. 5:12; 6:12-16; Eph. 2:11; Col. 2:11.) Dogs were regarded as unclean animals (Matt. 7:6; Rev. 22:15). Gentiles were considered unclean and were therefore called dogs by the Jews. Paul retorted on the Judaizers by using their own epithet. Peter spoke of those who have been exposed to a full human understanding of spiritual things—the coming of Christ, His substitutionary death, etc. After they heard these things, they turned from them and went back, thus evidencing that they were apostates. The latter end of those persons is worse than their beginning. Peter compared them to a dog returning to its vomit and a hog wallowing in the mud (II Pet. 2:20-22). This is not to say that some who are loving darkness and hating light (John 3:19) are not God's elect, but it is a Biblical fact that God's love must be poured out in the elect by the Spirit of regeneration before they can reciprocate by loving God. The marvel is not that God hates some, but that He loves any of us. Jesus Christ represented the Divine Being as the Father who yearned for the return of the prodigal, the good Shepherd who goes after the lost sheep until it is found, and the good Samaritan who saw His own lying in his wounds and came to save him at His own expense.

Those who believe in universal redemption or universal atonement are in error for the following reasons:

1. An atonement that fails to atone for all that God purposed is of no value. In His redemptive work, Jesus Christ did not make provision for all people without exception.

2. A redemption that comes short of delivering all for whom it was intended is worthless. Jesus Christ did not purpose to redeem all.

3. A sacrifice that does not release all for whom it was offered is invalid.

4. A reconciliation that does not reconcile all for whom it was decreed is deficient.

If particular redemption is denied, on what ground do unbelievers die in their sins? Surely no one would be so bold and foolish as to say that Christ died for their sins which were expiated in the death of Jesus Christ. That would be double jeopardy. Worse yet, it would be a denial of Christ's infinite sacrifice. Scripture teaches that Christ's death and advocacy are of the same extent. Both those who teach free will and those who teach free grace limit redemption. Redemption is limited, but we must discern where it is limited. Those who advocate universal redemption limit its value. Those who assert that redemption is restricted to those the Father chose and gave to Christ in the eternal covenant of grace restrict redemption to the elect. This latter belief does not limit its value but its extent. Thus, the redemptive work of Christ is not devaluated. The truth of particular redemption can be meaningless only if there is incongruity between "died for" and the limited object, "the elect." Since Christ died as a substitute, His redemption is not meaningless. As a result, no individual can say, "Christ died for all mankind."

The teaching of universal redemption contradicts all the major fundamental principles and characteristics of God:

1. Universal redemption would be contrary to God's purpose, because He could not say, "My purpose will be established, And I will accomplish all My good pleasure" (Is. 46:10 NASB).

2. Universal redemption would discredit God's wisdom, because He would have formed a redemption that fails to accomplish its intended conclusion.

3. Universal redemption would revoke God's love, because it would oppose what the Scripture says: "Jacob have I loved, but Esau have I hated" (Rom. 9:13).

4. Universal redemption would invalidate God's justice, because it would make God guilty of double jeopardy. If God paid for the sins of every person without exception and some are in hell today, they would be paying throughout eternity for their sins when Jesus Christ would have already paid for them.

5. Universal redemption would negate God's power, because failure must be from either want of will, purpose, or power. Since Arminians say God's will is that all

without exception be saved, they attribute the failure to want of power.

6. Universal redemption would nullify God's immutability, because His love would turn to hatred for the unbelievers who die in their sins. That would make God mutable, but God is constant. He is always the same.

7. Universal redemption would negate grace, because God's love would have motivated Him to die for all without exception and yet withhold grace from some.

8. Universal redemption would deny the death of Jesus Christ, because He would have died in vain for some. It would separate His death from His intercession, but those for whom He died equal in number those for whom He intercedes.

The Scriptural teaching concerning God and the order in which He works salvation follows:

1. God purposed to save some. He was the ransom for many, not all (Eph. 1:4; II Tim. 1:9).

2. God purposed to redeem those He purposed to save (I Pet. 1:18-21).

3. He purposed to regenerate those He purposed to redeem (John 3:8; Titus 3:5).

4. He purposed that those He regenerates will believe (Acts 13:48).

5. God purposed that those who believe will be holy (Eph. 1:4; I Thess. 4:3-7; Heb. 12:14).

6. God purposed that those who will be holy shall persevere (Matt. 10:22; Heb. 10:39).

7. God purposed that those who persevere shall be glorified (Rom. 8:30).

All this was in God's mind eternally at once. He does not think successively but simultaneously. As these things were simultaneously in his mind in eternity, the execution of them will be in the same order in time.

God has a special purpose but universal power. He gave Jesus Christ universal power in order that His purpose might be brought to fruition (John 17:3). God's universal power enables Him to accomplish His eternal purpose. The possibility that man could prevent God from accomplishing His purpose would signify that man is bigger than God, thus humanizing God and elevating man. Arminians assume that they work in conjunction with the grace of God in the regeneration of a passive sinner. Their idol, "free will," is extolled because they attribute free will as the initiating act that causes God to respond to man's act. Hence, the Arminian idea is that if the sinner will come to Christ in faith, grace attains its purpose; but if he wills to resist, the purpose of God is defeated.

The following are some questions that prove the fallacy of Arminian answers to them:

1. When two men hear the same message (the proclamation of the gospel) and only one is saved but the other dies in his sins, did God purpose to save only one? The Arminian answers, "No, because the same operation of the Spirit always accompanies the word." In contrast to the Arminian answer, Paul addressed Christians when he stated that the gospel came to them in power, in the Holy Spirit, and in much assurance

(I Thess. 1:5). The same word preached does not enter with power into the unregenerate person.

2. Did God work more powerfully in the heart of one than the other? The Arminian answers negatively. On the contrary, one hears, has assurance, appropriates what he has heard, and is active for the things of the Lord; but the other hears, goes away, and shortly forgets what he heard. To the person whose heart has been prepared by the grace of God in regeneration, the word enters his heart, remains, and works effectually in those who believe (I Thess. 2:13).

3. Does God open the heart of one person and not the heart of another? The Arminian reply completely ignores the Scripture by saying, "No, that would destroy the freedom of the will." But the Biblical answer is recorded in Acts 16:14. Neither Lydia nor Paul but God opened her heart, and the result was that she received the message. However, God did not open the heart of Simon Magus (Acts 8).

4. Who makes men to differ? The Arminian answers, "It always remained in the power of free will to reject grace that is given and to refuse that which follows; grace is no almighty action of God which free will cannot resist." In contrast, the Bible states that God makes the difference (I Cor. 4:7).

5. How does God subdue the will of the sinner? The Arminian answers that man is neither a robot nor a puppet on a string. The Arminian does not recognize that there is a vast difference between a depraved sinner and a robot. The sinner can move, and his will acts; but all its actions are wrong. Christ said that people will not come to Him that they might have life (John 5:40). One who does not believe that the will of man is depraved does not believe in depravity; and if he does not believe in depravity, he does not believe in grace. God does not overpower the sinner's will as a policeman

would overpower a criminal and put him in jail against his will. The first work of the Holy Spirit in the passive sinner is to impart the principle of life in regeneration (John 3:1-8), called "the Spirit of grace" (Heb. 10:29). Hence, the regenerated man, that person into whose heart God has imparted the principle of life, possesses a new heart, a new spirit, and a new understanding. This may be called the beginning of God's good work in His own (Phil. 1:6); and what God has begun in His own, He will bring to fruition.

The Biblical reply to opposition to irresistible grace is portrayed in the following truths:

1. God's purpose guarantees love.

2. Election is the proof of God's love.

3. Christ's incarnation and death are manifestations of God's love.

4. Regeneration enables the loved to experience God's love.

5. Glorification is the climax or the ultimate fruition of God's love in the elect.

The will of man makes absolutely no contribution to the good work by the sovereign God. Man is passive to that which is spiritual. Internal grace is the operation of God. Therefore, this operation of God gives new light to the understanding (Eph. 1:18) and new thinking which produces new affections (Col. 3:2). We love what God loves, and we hate what God hates. God's hatred is as perfect as His love; when we hate what God hates, our hatred is as perfect as our love when we are loving the things God loves. The operation of God gives new inclinations to the will. Our preferences are no longer self-willed, but God's will is our desire. The Biblical order is God first, others second, and self last.

The irresistibility of grace should not be viewed as violently beating down the will of man. But we cannot ignore the truth that no one can resist the will of God: "Then you will say to me: Why does He still find fault? for who has resisted [perfect active indicative of *anthistemi*, resist, oppose, set oneself against, or withstand] His will [*boulema*, purpose, desire, or intention]" (Rom. 9:19—translation). Acts 11:17 follows on the heels of Peter's statement about preaching to the Gentiles and proclaiming that God was doing for them what He had previously done for the Jews: "Since therefore God gave to them the same gift as also to us, who believed on the Lord Jesus Christ, who was I to be able to hinder [aorist active infinitive of *koluo*, to prevent, stop, or forbid] God?" (translation). No one can stop God's purpose with anyone. Grace cannot be stopped by a hard and rebellious heart, because the entrance of grace in regeneration makes the heart soft and receptive to truth and the will willing to obey truth. Therefore, Paul was severe, but he was also compassionate. Grace enters by the sovereign God's act, and by that act we are new people with new understanding, new thinking, and new desires.

11

NO JUDGMENT ON THOSE GOD LOVES

For God sent not the Son into the world in order that He may judge the world, but in order that the world may be saved through Him. The one believing because of Him is not being judged; the one not believing has been judged already, because he has not believed in the name of the unique Son of God. And this is the judgment, that the light has come into the world and men loved the darkness rather than the light; because their deeds were sinful. For everyone practicing evil things hates the light and does not come to the light, in order that his works may be exposed; but the one practicing the truth comes to the light, in order that his deeds may be revealed that they have been produced by God. —John 3:17-21 (translation)

The word "for" (*gar*) connects John 3:17 with the preceding verse. The aorist active indicative of *apostello*, which means to send forth, is a compound verb made up of *apo* and *stello.* It is used in the constative sense to show that it views the action in its entirety. God sent not the Son into (*eis*, accusative of extent) the world of mankind (*kosmos*) in order that He may judge (present active subjunctive of *krino*; this verb has a wide range of meaning, which can be reduced in our context to judge or condemn) the world of the elect (*kosmos*) but (*alla*, the strongest Greek adversative) in order that the world of the elect (*kosmos*) may be saved. The world of the elect is the subject of "saved" (*sothe*, aorist passive subjunctive of *sodzo*). The elect are saved through (*dia*, ablative of agency) the Son, Jesus Christ. The common interpretation of verse 17 is that Jesus Christ did not come the first time to judge, but He will judge when He comes the second time. However, He did judge at His first coming, manifested by His driving the money changers out of the temple.

In John 3:18, the person believing (*pisteuon*, present active participle of *pisteuo*) because of (*eis*, accusative of cause) Him is not being judged. The verb for judged is present passive indicative of *krino*, which means judge, condemn, or administer justice. This judgment is negated by the adverb *me*. In contrast to the one believing, the one not (*me*) believing (present active participle of *pisteuo*) stands judged (*kekritai*, perfect passive indicative of *krino*—completed action in past time with a resulting state of judgment—stands judged) already (*ede*, adverb), because (*hoti*, causal conjunction) in the past he refused to believe (perfect active indicative of *pisteuo*), with a resulting state of unbelief, in (*eis*, accusative of reference) the name (*onoma*, title or authority; but more than that, it refers to the Person whose name declares who He is) of the unique Son of God. Hence, unbelievers stand judged because they refuse to believe that Jesus Christ is the Person His name declares Him to be, the unique Son of God.

The only two major divisions of people in the world of mankind are believers and unbelievers. This eliminates the so-called third category composed of unbelievers who at one time were believers. Those who accept the false theory of the possibility of believers (Christians) becoming unbelievers (non-Christians) ask about those who believe for a brief time; and in time of trial, they become apostates (Luke 8:13). Their question drives persons interested in Biblical truth back to the two basic principles of John 3:1-21. Apart from a clear understanding of the difference between subjective and objective life, one will never be able to handle seemingly contradictory Scriptures.

Persons lacking the subjective life of the Spirit in regeneration may for a brief time believe with human faith (Luke 8:13). They may believe in the same manner as those who saw the miracles Christ performed (John 2:23-25); Simon Magus, who heard Philip's preaching and wanted to buy the power he saw demonstrated in Peter (Acts 8:12-25); those described in the Hebrew Epistle as turning back (Heb. 10:38, 39); or the demons (James 2:19). The major difference between the demons and religionists is that demons believe and shudder, and religionists believe but do not shudder. Believing apart from the regenerating Spirit is a faith that cannot endure the test.

One who consciously lays hold of Jesus Christ because he has been unconsciously laid hold of by the regenerating Holy Spirit has saving faith. The "spirit of faith" (II Cor. 4:13) is a part of the subjective life of the Spirit in regeneration (John 3:8); therefore, that which is a part cannot be the cause of the whole. Since no fact can be known before the existence of that fact, by the same logic, one cannot know by faith that he has been regenerated unless he has been regenerated: "Everyone believing that Jesus is the Christ has been born [perfect passive indicative of *gennao*, to be born] out of [*ek*, ablative of source] God, and everyone loving [present active participle nominative masculine singular of *agapao*] the One who gave birth [aorist active participle of *gennao*] is loving [present active indicative of *agapao*] the one who has been born [perfect passive participle of *gennao*] out of [*ek*, ablative of source] God" (I John 5:1—translation).

Faith apart from the Spirit of regeneration is nothing more than unregenerate human faith which can never be called God's gift of faith (Eph. 2:8), your most holy faith (Jude 20), or the faith of God's elect (Titus 1:1). The preposition *en*, instrumental of cause of John 3:15, and the preposition *eis*, the accusative of cause of John 3:16 and 18, signify, "because of Him [Christ]." Therefore, the elect are capable of objectively laying hold of Jesus Christ by faith; because having been legally crucified with Christ at Calvary, we have been subjectively laid hold of in regeneration. (See I John 5:9-13.)

Any person who cannot see that "born of God" precedes "believing" is either spiritually blind, or he is so filled with prejudice that he cannot see the forest of God's truth for the trees of human traditions and denominational customs. Simulation, which is the act or process of pretending, is currently popular. Pretentiousness creates an imaginary characteristic or plays the part of something that is unreal. A simulator is either a person or thing that simulates. Hence, some persons feign what they are not, and some machines simulate certain conditions for purposes of training or experimentation. We are made aware of these by the Space Program with which we have become familiar. Simulated diamonds to the untrained eye appear to be the genuine article. The average assembly member today is incapable of distinguishing a simulated assembly member from one who has been born out of God, because he has so little knowledge of Holy Scripture which enables one to make a righteous judgment according to God's word (John 7:24).

The generally accepted view of faith is that it is the instrument by which the sinner is united to Jesus Christ. Being united to Christ is understood by those who adopt that view to mean one has been born again. However, since saving faith is God's gift, the effect cannot affect or change the effect. Simply stated, saving faith is not the cause of itself. According to Scripture, no one can believe except by means of grace (Acts 18:27). Therefore, the "spirit of faith" which is a living faith (II Cor. 4:13) comes from the Spirit of regeneration (John 3:8). The unregenerate person does not possess a living faith. This raises an important question, How can a spiritually dead faith make one alive in Christ Jesus? Spiritual activity is as impossible for a person dead in trespasses and sins as physical activity is for one physically dead (Eph. 2:1; Heb. 9:14).

Order in salvation must be observed with reference to both God and man. This order is exemplified in the vessels of the tabernacle (Ex. 25-40) and in the offerings (Lev. 1-5). God's order is election, redemption, regeneration, and calling which brings faith into operation. However, man's order is reversed in his understanding. Man's order begins with God's effectual call which brought the "spirit of faith" into action. He is then made to realize that he could never have heard the call apart from regeneration. At this point, he learns that regeneration is the product of Christ's redemptive work at Calvary. Finally, he is taught by God that redemption is the fruit of Divine election. Election is the highest and faith is the lowest rung in the ladder of man's salvation from the curse and penalty of sin. If God began with man's faith, as most religionists teach, the ladder of salvation would be inverted. This would mean that man's faith would become the highest and God's sovereign choice would become the lowest in man's deliverance. That view of salvation is nothing short of blasphemy, because man would be deified and God would be humanized. Thus, the "worthless mind" is manifested (Rom. 1:28; II Thess. 2:11).

Modern-day psychology is one of Christianity's worst enemies. One of psychology's foundational principles is to give man self-esteem. Its philosophy is that when you destroy a man's self-respect by making him feel that by nature he is worthless because of depravity, he is driven to a reckless and sinful life.

Gospel regeneration is the next thing to the heretical teaching of baptismal regeneration. Used to support the supposition of gospel generation and based on John 3:18 are the following arguments and answers to them:

1. Those who believe in gospel regeneration affirm that without active faith one is condemned. They then question, How can a person be alive because of regeneration and condemned at the same time, since some claim that one must have life in order to believe?

Answer: (1) God chose the elect in eternity before He chooses them in time (Eph. 1:4; I Pet. 1:2). (2) God gave the elect to Christ in eternity before He gives them to Christ in time (John 17:6, 9, 11, 12; 24; 6:37). (3) Grace was given the elect in Christ before the times of ages (II Tim. 1:9), and it is brought to the elect in time (Titus 2:11-14). (4) The elect were justified on the foundation of Christ's redemptive work before they are justified in their consciousness by faith (Rom. 3:24-26; 5:1). (5) The elect were justified before God while they were the children of wrath (Eph. 2:1-3). Justification in the sight of God was on the ground of imputed righteousness, and justification by faith is on the premise of imparted righteousness. If this is difficult for you to understand, ask yourself the question, How could Jesus Christ be made a curse when He was perfect? Christ was made a curse, even though He was perfect, in order that the elect could have a justification before God while they were walking according to the spirit working in the sons of disobedience.

2. Those who believe in gospel regeneration argue that a person becomes a son of God by faith in Jesus Christ (Gal. 3:26). Therefore, they assume that one must hear the gospel, repent, and believe in order to become a regenerated son of God. They ask, what shall those who believe in a time lapse between regeneration and conversion do with Ephesians 1:13?

Answer: Anyone who teaches that an unregenerate person can believe on Christ and be saved (born of God) denies depravity. In the first place, regeneration and salvation are not synonymous terms. Regeneration is not the making of the old man into a better person; the Spirit produces a new creation (II Cor. 5:17; Eph. 2:10; John 6:63). On the other hand, one can be saved by faith (Luke 7:50), fire (I Cor. 3:15), preaching (I Cor. 1:21), endurance (Matt. 10:22), calling (Acts 2:21), Christ's life (Rom. 5:10), himself (Acts 2:40; I Tim. 4:16), through childbearing (I Tim. 2:15), through water (I Pet. 3:20), etc. In these matters, the word is a means of salvation (conversion experience), but it is not the means of life. The Scriptures are profitable for teaching, reproof, and instruction in righteousness; but the word of God does not make one alive in Jesus Christ. Furthermore, the word of God enables the passive person who has been made alive by the sovereign Spirit to know by his spiritual activity in his studying the Scriptures that he is alive in Christ (I John 5:13; I Thess. 1:5, 6; 2:13).

Both Paul and John were fathers with children (I Cor. 4:14-17; I John 2:1); but their fatherhood as servants was in relation to their teaching, not by their infusing the principle of life. As children of God, Christians have only one Father, our Father who is in heaven. Without subjective life by the sovereign Spirit, believing the objective message of Jesus Christ would be impossible. On the other hand, when a person is regenerated, failure to believe on Christ is impossible.

Paul's statement to the Galatians, "For you are all the sons [*huoi*, nominative masculine plural of *huios*, denotes dignity of relationship] of God, *dia tes pisteos en Christo Iesou*" (Galatians 3:26—translation), can mean we are the sons of God either "through the faithfulness in Christ Jesus" or "through the faith in Christ Jesus." Are we sons of God by Christ's faithfulness, or by our faithfulness? Paul was writing to Christians. Although either translation is grammatically correct, those who claim it means "faith in Christ Jesus" are forced to acknowledge that faith is the fruit of regeneration in the sense that it is part of the salvation which was planned by the Father, provided by Christ's death, and applied by the Holy Spirit. Anyone who believes that as the result of having been born of God through faith in Christ as his Savior, he has received His nature, and thus he loves God as well as all those who have been born of God, makes the effect the cause of the effect. That belief is as heretical as the assertion that by faith you breathe the Holy Spirit into your life, and He gives you spiritual life. In contrast, both repentance and faith are gifts of God which originate from the Holy Spirit in regeneration (Jer. 31:18, 19; Acts 11:18; Eph. 2:8; Phil. 1:29; II Tim. 2:25; Heb. 12:2).

God-given faith brings knowledge, affections, and will into humble submission to the one true and living God; and it submits to the provision made by God for man. Since faith is part of the new creation in Christ, the elect are not regenerated by faith; but the regenerated elect are saved through faith. Faith produces acts of grace, but not the disposition of grace. True faith makes all of life meaningful and draws us out of ourselves. Hence, the faith of God's elect leads to full knowledge of the truth according to godliness (*eusebeia*, reverential feeling, piety, and devotion to God). (See I Tim. 3:16; 4:7, 8; Titus 1:1.)

Faith is represented by religionists as being of human

origin. They claim it is the same kind as the human quality which causes one to put his money in a bank or his confidence in an airline when he takes his seat in an airplane. In this manner, sinners are told to transfer such belief from worldly objects to Jesus Christ, and the result will be the new birth. Therefore, under the emotional stimulus of mob psychology brought about by eloquent, forceful, and persuasive preachers, millions of people transfer their so-called trust to God, join assemblies, are baptized, and put to work. Since these methods have proved to be successful, who can question success? Being blinded by their human religion, they cannot see or understand that God argues against and condemns every religious system. In all human systems, more emphasis is placed on the method than the Savior; human means, than the Holy Spirit; human experiences and testimonies, than the word of God; numbers, than looking for Christ's sheep; entertaining the flesh, than appealing to those who have been made alive by regeneration; etc. The cardinal point to all this is that man's system is a work of merit, but God's work is one of grace. If man's faith saves his soul, what saves his body or perfects his salvation? If faith is nothing more than a human act, how can it be called "the faith of God's elect" (Titus 1:1)? Paul spoke of his apostleship as being for the purpose of "the faith of God's elect with a view to their full knowledge of truth according to godliness on the basis of hope of eternal life, which God who cannot lie promised before time began" (Titus 1:1, 2—translation).

The following are some characteristics of the two categories of mankind in John 3:17-21:

Believer	Unbeliever
1. Saved.	1. Lost
2. Because of Christ.	2. Because of depravity.
3. In a state of believing.	3. In a state of judgment.
4. Believes Christ is the Person His name declares Him to be.	4. Refuses to believe Christ is the Person His name declares Him to be.
5. Loves light.	5. Loves darkness.
6. Practices the truth.	6. Practices evil.
7. Comes to the light.	7. Hates the light.
8. Desires to have his deeds revealed.	8. Does not desire to have his evil deeds exposed.
9. Regenerated — This is the crucial point, because regeneration produces faith and a fruitful life.	9. Is not regenerated — This is the bottom line, because without the new birth he does not have God-given faith; hence, he lives a life of sin.

The believer's believing (present active participle of *pisteuo*) (John 3:18), not being judged (present passive indicative of *krino*) (John 3:18), practicing truth (present active participle of *poieo*) (John 3:21), and coming to the light (present middle indicative of *erchomai*) (John 3:21) are all climaxed (the highest point because it points to the sovereign God) with a perfect passive participle of *ergadzomai* (John 3:21), which means the believer's present believing, not being judged, practicing truth, and coming to the light have been produced by God (Eph. 2:10; Phil. 1:6; 2:13). The believer can no more shut up the book of experience than he can the book of God's revelation. He believes, lives, and speaks the truth.

On the other hand, the unbeliever is not believing (present active participle of *pisteuo*) (John 3:18), has been judged (perfect passive indicative of *krino*, in a state of judgment) (John 3:18), has not believed (perfect active indicative of *pisteuo*, is in a state of not believing) (John 3:18), loved (aorist active indicative of *agapao*, used in the constative sense, viewing the action in its entirety) darkness because his deeds have always been (imperfect active indicative of *eimi*—description of what was going on in past time) evil (John 3:19), practices (present active participle of *prasso*) evil things (John 3:20), hates (present active indicative of *miseo*) the light (John 3:20), and does not come (present active indicative *erchomai*) to the light that his works may be exposed (John 3:20). Thus, he manifests a continuous life of sin. One's life of sin is not because of man's total inability, seeing that he has the ability to sin. His life of sin is because of his total spiritual inability, which includes his mind, heart, and will. He does not need some unusual exertion to do evil, since he is naturally inclined to practice evil. There is a tendency in man for what is easy and natural to become habitual. Thus, the unregenerate person goes from smaller sins to greater sins. The greatest sins are done under the cloaks of religious systems.

That which has been born out of the flesh is the willing instrument of sin for the reason that it is in a state of sinfulness

SCRIPTURE INDEX

John (Cont'd)

John (Cont'd)

Books And Pamphlets By W. E. Best

Mailing address for obtaining copies of the books and pamphlets:

W. E. Best Book Missionary Trust
P. O. Box 34904
Houston, Texas 77234-4904 USA

BOOKS

Regeneration And Conversion

Studies In The Person And Work Of Jesus Christ

God Forgives Sinners

Free Grace Versus Free Will

The Saviour's Definite Redemption
(*Studies in Isaiah 53*)

The Church—Her Authority & Mission

Christ Emptied Himself

Christ Could Not Be Tempted

God Is Love

Diminishing Spirituality In Local Churches
(*Studies in Revelation 2 & 3*)

Eternity And Time

Woman—Man's Completion

Justification Before God (Not By Faith)

God's Longsuffering Is Salvation

The Most Neglected Chapter In The Bible
(*Romans 9*)

Life Brought To Light

Christ's Kingdom Is Future — Vol. I
(*The King's Genealogy*)

Christ's Kingdom Is Future — Vol. II
(*Introduction Of The King*)

Christ's Kingdom Is Future — Vol. III
(*Formation Of The King's Bride*)

BOOKS (continued)

A Comprehensive View Of Romans — Vol. I

The Born-Again Phenomenon
(A Cover-Up For Heresy)

Simple Faith *(A Misnomer)*

PAMPHLETS

Honoring The True God

No Proper Name Given To Christ's Assembly

God's Eternal Decree

PAMPHLETS IN SPANISH

Honrando Al Dios Verdadero

BOOKS IN SPANISH

Vida Sacada A Luz

La Libre Gracia En Contra Del Libre Albedrío

Dios Perdona Pecadores

Dios Es Amor

La Redención Definida Del Salvador
(Estudios En Isaías 53)

Cristo No Pudo Ser Tentado

Other books and pamphlets will be available in Spanish in 1993.